BACK ON TRACK

DAVID GILLICK is one of Ireland's most successful athletes. He helped push the boundaries of sprinting by winning two European Championships over 400m while consistently competing with some of the fastest one-lap athletes in the world, resulting in Irish records and a 6th place finish in the World Championships. After retiring from athletics, David found some hidden talents and interests. From full-time corporate employment to the *Celebrity MasterChef* kitchen, he has gone on to follow his passions of fitness, food and promoting a healthy lifestyle. David's first cookbook, *David Gillick's Kitchen*, was a bestseller and he now runs his own business as an active food writer, media contributor, speaker and health advocate. He currently resides in Dublin with his wife and young family.

BACK ON TRACK

EAT, MOVE, THINK AND REST YOUR WAY TO YOUR HAPPIEST, HEALTHIEST SELF

DAVID GILLICK

GILL BOOKS

Gill Books
Hume Avenue
Park West
Dublin 12
www.gillbooks.ie

Gill Books is an imprint of M.H. Gill and Co.

978 07171 8156 8

Designed by www.grahamthew.com
Text edit by Orla Neligan
Copy edit by Susan McKeever
Proofread by Jane Rogers
Indexed by Eileen O'Neill
Photographed by Leo Byrne
Styled by Orla Neligan of Cornershop Productions
www.cornershopproductions.com
Assisted by Clare Wilkinson

PROPS
Meadows & Byrne: Dublin T: 01 2804554 E: info@meadowsandbyrne.ie;
www.meadowsandbyrne.com
Marks & Spencer: Unit 1–28, Dundrum Town Centre, Dublin 16.
T: 01 2991300; W: www.marksandspencer.ie
Article Dublin: Powerscourt Townhouse, South William Street, Dublin 2.
T: 01 6799268; E:items@articledublin.com; W: www.articledublin.com
Dunnes Stores: 46–50 South Great Georges Street, Dublin 2. T: 1890
253185; www.dunnesstores.com
TK Maxx: The Park, Carrickmines, Dublin 18.
T: 01 2074798; W: www.tkmaxx.ie
House of Fraser: Dundrum, Dublin 14.
T: 01 2991400; W: houseoffraser.co.uk
Kathryn Davey Fabrics: kathryndavey.com
Eyewear by Optica, Dublin

Printed by Printer Trento Srl, Italy
This book is typeset in 9 on 13 point, Sofia Pro.

The paper used in this book comes from the wood pulp of managed
forests. For every tree felled, at least one tree is planted, thereby
renewing natural resources.

A CIP catalogue record for this book is available from the British Library.

5 4 3 2 1

ACKNOWLEDGEMENTS

I'm not going to lie! After my first book, I said: never again. Believe me, a lot of work goes into getting a book on a shelf. If it wasn't for Sarah Liddy, this book would have never materialised. Sarah, thank you for annoying me and also giving me the confidence and belief to start writing the book.

Massive thank you to Orla Neligan, along with Clare Wilkinson, who styled all the beautiful pictures in this book but also to Orla for extracting my story, which was not an easy thing to do. I appreciate your patience on some difficult personal topics.

I'm delighted with the images in this book. They capture a lot of my personality and without Leo Byrne's brilliance and fun attitude, it simply wouldn't have become a reality.

Food is a huge part of this book and Clare Ann O'Keefe gave so much of her time in helping me to better myself in the kitchen and improve my knowledge around food. Straight away, you understood my ethos on food and healthy eating.

Huge thanks to the amazing people at Gill Books who worked hard on my behalf to make this book a reality. Thanks for making me feel like part of your team and giving me the belief that it would be a success.

Finally, to Charlotte, Oscar and ... (bump), you are what matters most. I'm very lucky.

CONTENTS

RECIPES

INTRODUCTION

As an elite 400m sprint athlete I have a string of successes under my belt. I finished sixth in the world in 2009, won the European Indoor Championships in 2005 and 2007, beat some of the best athletes in the world and realised my dream of competing at the 2008 Beijing Olympics. For as long as I can remember I have been an achiever, wearing my 'stop-at-nothing' armour with the prize being the Olympics. And yet, on a Sunday in 2015, I found myself sitting at my kitchen table in Dublin contemplating suicide.

I had spent the best part of the two previous years since my retirement from athletics with the handbrake on. I had become disengaged, moody and deeply unhappy, finally being diagnosed with depression earlier that year. I looked across the table at my wife Charlotte, who was eight months pregnant, and realised I could not bring a baby into the world with this 'head' on my shoulders; something had to change. This was my eureka moment, my absolute rock bottom.

In late 2010 I had made the decision to move to America to give myself the best opportunity to train for the 2012 London Olympics. Within two months of arriving I suffered a calf injury that would be the start of my athletic demise. The scene in America was tough: I was the only white European among a group of athletes who had no interest in socialising. I was lonely and isolated and yet determined that putting myself among some of the best sprinters in the world would be the best environment for me – a knee-jerk reaction to a season that hadn't gone so well. I soon returned to the UK to prepare for the Olympics but found I was trailing behind my fellow athletes. The injury had knocked my self-esteem, which fed my performance anxiety. Each time I hit the track was an attempt to replicate my personal best and the success I once had. I was pushing 30: younger athletes were passing me by and I didn't like it. A toxic inner voice was bombarding me with undermining questions: Why wasn't I as fast as these guys? Why couldn't I hit my time markers? After all, I had finished sixth in the World Championships. Shouldn't I be leading the pack? I started to overanalyse everything and soon my sleep, eating habits and mental health suffered. My meals became a finely deconstructed calorie count, my sleep was disturbed, my relationships were fraught with tension. I had learned about defeats but not about how to deal with a long-term injury and could not accept where it had left me. I didn't trust my body and it showed on the track and at home.

Injury struck again in February 2012. My Olympic dream was over.

The negative thinking exploded and the self-bashing trickled into other aspects of my life. My brain was trained to win and to focus on the physical element of my performance. Never did I consider how my mental health and attitude was affecting my ability to perform. As I soon realised, if your head isn't in the game, you've lost before you've started.

Confused and a little beaten, I moved to Australia in the post-Olympic months for a year in an attempt at a fresh start and to enjoy training life. It was a great year but also one filled with self-doubt and worry about what I was going to do with my life. I was crippled with insecurity and dread at the prospect of life without athletics.

They say professional athletes die twice, retirement being the first of their 'deaths'. The structured routine and vigorous training is no longer necessary, the adulation and attention disappears. Sponsors fall away. You're the man. And then, you're not. What you are left with is the battle scars, the memories and yourself, scrambling to relearn how to function in normal society and too much time to think about it. My long-term plan had been to finish up in the Rio Olympics in 2016. Instead, I found myself facing the difficult decision to retire soon after returning to Dublin in 2013, a decision that I feel I had no control over – I knew that my running career would probably end in my mid-thirties but I wasn't even 30 yet! I told myself I was taking time to 'figure things out' following the injury but it didn't last long. Uncomfortable with the idea of sitting with myself, I soon found a job with a sports performance company but I missed everything about athletics: the identity, the buzz, the goal, training with my friends, the adrenaline hit. I missed being scraped off the track on a Tuesday morning and that feeling of achievement. Soon 'athletics' became a dreaded word. I couldn't talk, read about or watch athletics. I stopped running and became resentful. If I hadn't started running in the first place, I wouldn't be in this mess. It didn't take long before all exercise was shelved and the comfort eating started.

I would stop at garages and sit in the car gorging on muffins while somewhere in the back of my mind I'd be promising myself a run later to try to assuage the guilt. The run never happened – not that night, nor the following day or week. I devoured vats of ice cream and packs of biscuits in one sitting. I retreated into my own home and mind; afraid to meet people in case they would ask me what I was doing with myself. I'd been successful on the athletics track so surely whatever I did next would have to be equally dazzling! I started to sink into a hole from which I couldn't emerge. I would spend hours on social media comparing myself to other athletes, finally peeling myself away from my phone with my self-confidence on the floor. The time, energy and focus you put into your athletic career exceeds almost anything else you do in life, swallowing your identity whole. It also exposes the crudely simple rhetoric of sport: Winning is good, and promises joy. Losing is bad, and brings strife. Vulnerability doesn't come into it. I had left my identity on the track and had no idea who I was. I struggled to define my self-worth apart from my athletic career; after all it's easier to say 'I *am* an athlete' than 'I *was* an athlete'.

I developed psoriasis all over my body, night sweats that were so bad the entire mattress was soaked through. I became moody and fractious, arguing over trivial things. One morning after a meltdown over something unimportant, I stormed out of the house and into my car. When I finally looked at my phone an hour later there were 20 missed calls from Charlotte, my then fiancée, desperate to know if I was okay since she had heard on the radio that a person had died by suicide after jumping from a bridge on the M50 and she was convinced it was me. I was not comfortable with who I was and where I was but I wasn't asking for help. Depression is a dirty word in the locker room; how could I be depressed considering my success? It was the deepest, darkest, quietest place I've ever been. Finally, on that Sunday in December, I suffered a panic attack and made a phone call, the most important phone call of my life: I asked for help.

From that December three years ago until now, I have been clawing my way back. I started to get better when I accepted I had a problem and started talking about how I felt; when I changed my habits and listened to what my body needed. I have learned that those moments that threaten to unglue us are often the ones that help us understand our worth. I have discovered that my mind is the most important tool in my toolbox. The stories I

tell myself affect every decision I make. I have realised that for peak performance you need a balance between four pillars: Mindset, Movement, Relaxation and Diet. Through the help of a counsellor and by making small changes in various areas of my life, I have rediscovered my love for exercise. I have remembered how much I love food and cooking. I have understood the importance of sleep and downtime to my overall wellbeing and I have learned to be aware of those moments when I am *mindful*, not *mind full*. I have bad days but in general I have found a better me, one I am happy to spend time with.

THE BOOK

When I look back at myself post retirement all I see is a busy fool. I was working full-time and doing extra gigs at the weekends, I had very little quality time with my family and was constantly tired with little or no downtime. So I went back to something I used at the height of my athletic career – the wheel of life technique. Back then, I was working with sports psychologists who trained us to use this technique to map out key areas of our lives into percentages using a big circle. As an athlete, 80 per cent of my time was spent training, with the remaining 20 per cent split between my family and friends. Not a very healthy balance, but normal

enough for a career athlete. However, when I retired and started a 'normal' career, the 80 per cent was just transferred to work. Still no balance. So I looked at the wheel and saw how I prioritised my time and what was suffering, and this, along with other changes, helped create some balance in my life.

In today's instant-gratification world, good health is now a major fashion trend so that everywhere we look we see quick fixes – people championing the virtues of this or that life-changing diet or new fitness regime. Social media is breeding a culture of comparison that is unhealthy and detrimental to people's mental health. I now realise that we can't change the modern landscape but we can change how we interact with it. Your body and your mind are interconnected and should be seen as a whole, which is why you need to take a helicopter view of your health.

There is no one way of living a healthy life. Exercise and diet have long been touted as the panacea for ill-health and it can be confusing with many of us thinking: what's best for me? Or, where do I start? While the old adage that food and exercise are fundamental to good health certainly holds weight, it fails to recognise the importance of other pillars in our lives.

The idea for this book was born from my own story and a desire to share my experience: my career as an elite athlete, subsequent spiral into depression and journey back to a better way of living. I'm now certain that it isn't simply one thing that helped me back, but a combination. I have my better-living toolbox sorted and I want to share it with people. It doesn't matter if you've never run in your life, what we have in common is that we're all human. The toolbox takes the holistic approach, which is the winning formula. At its heart is a simple premise: good health requires creating balance in those four key areas of your life:

1. **MINDSET**
2. **MOVEMENT**
3. **REST**
4. **DIET**

I have shared tips and methods for creating that balance but it's designed to complement *your* life, so I would encourage you to only choose elements that work for *you*. It's a 'life' plan that is simple, accessible and easy to follow. No short cuts, no miracle pills; you simply begin to make small changes, with the big picture in mind.

1. MINDSET

A set of beliefs or a way of thinking
that determines one's behaviour,
outlook and mental attitude

We often underestimate how powerful our minds really are. It's our inner voice and the language it uses that really determines how we approach things in our lives. Mindset is essentially a set of attitudes fuelled by our internal dialogue and when we change it to one of 'growth' as opposed to 'fixed', we can alter the course of our lives. Many of us stunt our growth by having a fixed mindset with limiting beliefs. And, since our states of mind feed our inner belief systems, which form habits and ultimately, our lifestyles, getting that right is crucial for attaining good health. Have you ever found yourself saying something like, 'I can't lose weight, nothing ever works' or 'I hate exercise, I'm just not sporty'? This is an example of a fixed mindset – by changing this to something like, 'I've struggled to lose weight in the past but that's because I hadn't found the method that worked for me.'

GROWTH VERSUS FIXED MINDSET

THE FIXED MINDSET

* Avoids challenges
* Sees effort as fruitless
* Ignores useful feedback
* Is discouraged by mistakes.

THE GROWTH MINDSET

* Embraces challenges
* Sees consistent effort as vital
* Is open to constructive challenge
* Sees mistakes as opportunities.

How do we begin to make those mental changes?

THE FIXED MINDSET assumes that our basic characteristics such as talent or intelligence are static and cannot be changed in any meaningful way.

THE GROWTH MINDSET assumes that there are opportunities to grow, that you can learn new skills, ask for help and develop yourself, and that failure is a springboard for growth.

FOSTERING A GROWTH MINDSET

In his book *The Chimp Paradox*, leading sports psychologist Steve Peters talks about athletes taming their 'inner chimp' – that toxic voice on your shoulder spinning the negative yarn, which isn't just reserved for athletes but affects everyone. According to Peters, success goes hand-in-hand with happiness and confidence. If you suffer from unhelpful feelings of anxiety, your chimp is in control, so learning to recognise the difference between your chimp and yourself (or your fixed and growth mindset) is an important part of rewiring your brain to think positively.

The following are examples of the type of toxic voice that can create a fixed mindset:

* **Negative self-talk**
* **Irrational thoughts**
* **Lack of confidence**
* **Catastrophising everything**
* **Concentrating on what other people think of you.**

Naming your chimp can be a means of detaching yourself from it and challenging the annoying voice. My chimp, nicknamed Chopper, would usually visit before a big race when my anxiety levels were ramped up. I would challenge it or distract myself using various techniques I had learned:

* **I'd write down all the negative thoughts in my head, then rip up the paper and throw it in the bin.**
* **I'd write down all the positives – good training sessions, good races, results, etc.**
* **I made a video clip of my best races and put music to it – watching it gave me instant confidence.**

When anxiety strikes I now use the 3D technique:

DISTRACTION
TURN ON MUSIC, GET UP AND DO SOMETHING, WIND THE CAR WINDOW DOWN.

DISTANCE
I DISTANCE MYSELF FROM THAT VOICE IN MY HEAD – IT'S CHOPPER SPEAKING, NOT ME.

DISPUTE
BECAUSE IT'S CHOPPER AND NOT ME, I CAN DISPUTE WHAT HE IS SAYING.

But in the last few years Chopper was very much in charge. I didn't have the emotional bank or capacity to challenge him and he did a lot of damage.

Nowadays, he's a lot quieter but still needs reassurance from time to time.

Carol Dweck, a professor of psychology at Stanford University in California, has proved that those who apply a growth mindset suffer less stress and anxiety and enjoy long-term achievement and higher self-esteem. It follows that much of our behaviour and capacity for happiness is linked to these two mindsets. **You can't fix a problem with the same mindset that got you there**. Author Wallace D. Wattles may have put it best when he said, 'Whatever you habitually think yourself to be, that you are.'

Manage your self-talk using the REM technique.

RECOGNISE
BECOME AWARE OF YOUR INTERNAL DIALOGUE.

EVALUATE
IS IT POSITIVE OR NEGATIVE? WHAT IS THE CONSISTENCY OF YOUR THOUGHTS?

MODIFY
MAKE CHANGES –
IF THE TALK IS CONSTANTLY NEGATIVE, TRY TO CHANGE IT.

IDENTIFYING YOUR 'WHY?'

Growing up I knew I had a talent: I could run fast. It wasn't until my teenage years that I realised it could be a career. I didn't want to always wonder what my life might have been like as an athlete, I wanted to be that athlete with no regrets. That was my personal 'why?' **Your 'why' is the purpose or the belief that motivates you to achieve.** It could be to provide for your family or for yourself, to improve your health, run a marathon, lose weight or de-stress: we all have hopes, dreams and intentions but for many, fear of change or failure prevents us from taking the leap.

In my experience, change is usually something that is worth doing and you are the only person who can take ownership of it. When I was feeling my worst, ego was my biggest obstacle, driving a lot of bad decisions and suppressing the good ones. I found it hard to say 'no' to anyone, I was burnt out, run down, sleeping badly and too tired to train, eat well or hold proper conversations. When I realised there was no real value in anything I was doing I had to stop and ask myself, 'What's important?' I've definitely learned more from those 'dark' days – those 'failed' moments – than the successful ones. It's so easy to focus on the negatives or the things you didn't do or should have done; the result is you

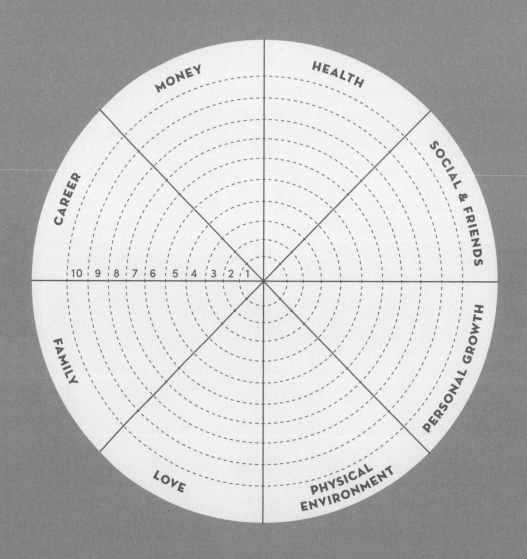

forget to focus on what makes you *you*! So it's important to check in with yourself now and again and a great way of doing that is using the wall of belief. Ask yourself WHY you want to do something. WHAT are your superpowers? WHAT is important to you? Are you WHERE you want to be? WHAT are your opportunities for growth? Knowing the WHY will help you figure out the WHAT and the HOW.

The wheel of life is a useful tool that measures how satisfied you are with your life. Draw a circle and divide it into eight slices (like a cake). Give each slice a label. You could divide it into things like career, money, social, personal growth, physical environment, health, etc. You can change the labels to reflect what is important to you, but I have given some examples on the opposite page. Give each area a score out of 10 with 0 being least satisfied and 10 being very satisfied. When you have scored all areas, connect the lines to form the inner wheel. This will give you a visual balance of your life as it is right now.

Once you have identified the areas you'd like to improve, it's time to start setting goals around them.

GOALS WITHOUT PLANS ARE WISHES

Starting out, I had a very fixed mindset. I rarely asked myself, 'How do I get to that goal?' or 'How do I build resilience and confidence?' When I did, I would hear that 'fixed' voice – Chopper – loud and clear: 'You're Irish, you can't sprint.' It wasn't until I won my first medal that I gained some confidence. I began making concrete plans and trusting them. If I wanted to get to the Olympics what did I need to do? Could I eat 15 good meals a week, get eight hours' sleep a night and work with a strength and conditioning coach? Put simply, I had a plan for maybe reaching my goal.

When setting your own goals, it might be useful to consider the SMART technique, which will help add structure and track-ability to your goals instead of leaving them as vague resolutions.

SPECIFIC
YOUR GOAL SHOULD BE CLEAR. WHAT DO YOU WANT TO DO? WHY IS IT IMPORTANT? WHO IS INVOLVED? WHERE IS IT LOCATED? WHICH RESOURCES ARE INVOLVED?

MEASURABLE
YOUR GOALS SHOULD BE TANGIBLE SO YOU CAN TRACK YOUR PROGRESS.

ACHIEVABLE
YOUR GOALS SHOULD BE ATTAINABLE.

RELEVANT
ENSURE YOUR GOAL MATTERS TO YOU AND IS WORTHWHILE.

TIME-BOUND
EVERY GOAL NEEDS A DEADLINE TO HELP YOU FOCUS.

Some examples of smart goals are: lose a stone in weight in the next three months, do a 20-minute run three times a week, run a 5K by the end of the month, eat breakfast Monday to Friday, turn my phone off in the evenings and play with my kids.

I would often have ten things I wanted to do but using this method really helped me focus on executing one single thing well. The next step was achieving it with a clear plan.

Start by asking yourself the questions on the opposite page.

CLEAR INTENTIONS – THE SECRET INGREDIENT

Goal, target, plan, intention – whatever you want to call it, it's a destination, somewhere you want to go. I prefer the term 'intention' as it feels more like a choice I am making without stress about an expectation that may not be met. Having clarity of mind and being focused propels us forward, allowing us to meet those intentions. Intent is the secret ingredient for attaining even the smallest of achievements with ease. And being realistic about our intentions or goals gives us a better chance of achieving them.

1

WHAT ARE YOUR VALUES, THE THINGS YOU FIND IMPORTANT IN HOW YOU LIVE AND WORK?

Examples can include accountability, belonging, commitment, excellence, faith, health, perfection and security.

2

WHAT ARE YOUR INTERESTS?

Examples can include sports, current affairs, history, reading, cinema and cookery.

3

WHAT TYPE OF PERSONALITY DO YOU HAVE?

Are you an introvert or an extrovert? Do you prefer team sports or individual pursuits? Are you competitive or a perfectionist? Are you naturally organised or chaotic?

4

WHAT ARE YOUR SKILLS?

Examples can include listening, cooking, being organised, being creative, looking after people or working well in a team.

5

WHAT ARE YOUR MOTIVATORS?

Examples can include health, appearance, being able to do more, self-esteem, family, money and success.

6

NOW SET A GOAL THAT MOTIVATES YOU. WRITE IT DOWN.

7

MAKE AN ACTION PLAN AND STICK WITH IT.

We've all been in the position of aiming too high only to fall at the first hurdle, so choosing ten things to do might be difficult to manage. Instead, ask yourself what really matters to you and when you can do it. Consider what you can do this week or even today. If you focus on the short-term process, the long-term goal will look after itself. And remember, there are no dead ends, just re-directions.

MAKING A PLAN FOR YOUR LIFESTYLE

Whenever I give a talk I always ask the audience to open the calendars on their phones and look at how many activities they have included for themselves in a week. Most people will say none. One of the most effective tools for cultivating a better mindset and lifestyle for me has been making a weekly plan, including some 'me-time'. Routine was always important to me while training. When I retired, I struggled to find that same sense of direction: I would wake and go to sleep at different times every day; I was always fatigued and as a result made poor food and lifestyle choices. I soon realised I need to create my own routine.

Waking and going to sleep at the same time each day is paramount – this sets my body clock for the day and culti-vates equilibrium. Every Friday, I take a half-hour to plan the following week and I include everything in that plan; from the times I get up and go to bed, to exercise, collecting my son Oscar from crèche and mealtimes.

Start with the non-negotiables – those events that don't get sacrificed for anything. For me, it's my run. Next, factor in everyone in your life who relies on you for something: kids, spouse, friends or parents. Everything goes into the plan: your work life, your partner's work life, meetings, dropping and collecting kids from school, shopping, meeting friends and activities scheduled over the weekend. Factoring in what I call the 'big rocks' first was instrumental in my recovery. In other words, make a list of the most important things and do them first: the tough phone call, the meeting you've been avoiding, the spin class you've missed – whatever the 'rock' you face, it'll be much harder to accomplish later in the day.

THE POWER OF HABIT

While it can be easy to start something new and to get into the habit of doing it, the difficulty is making it consistent. A study by Phillippa Lally, a health psychology researcher at University College London, examined the habits of 96 people over a 12-week period. She discovered that it took on average 66 days for a new behaviour to become automatic – an important fact to remember when we're embarking on any new regimes. She also found that 'missing one opportunity to perform the behaviour did not materially affect the habit formation process.' In other words, **building habits is not an all-or-nothing process and allows for deviation.** We're allowed to mess up now and again. This was important to me when starting to reclaim a healthier lifestyle.

Guilt is a powerful and wasted emotion; it serves no purpose. If you don't get out for your run or you end up eating that bar of chocolate, forgive yourself, give yourself permission to make mistakes and develop better strategies for getting back on track. **The important thing is you're committed to the process and not the quick fix.** Forming habits take time but there is great freedom in understanding that habits can change – we are not slaves to the bad ones; we have the ability to remake them. And one way behaviour can become habitual is through repetition.

This is where your plan comes in, using it to incorporate the three Rs of habit formation – Reminder, Routine and Reward – to form positive behaviour and actions.

R **REMINDER**
THE TRIGGER THAT STARTS THE HABIT (E.G. SET AN ALARM TO GO FOR A WALK, OR A NOTE OR AN OBJECT LEFT SOMEWHERE TO JOG YOUR MEMORY).

R **ROUTINE**
THE ACTION OR HABIT YOU TAKE (E.G. GOING FOR A WALK).

R **REWARD**
IF THE REWARD IS POSITIVE YOU'LL HAVE A DESIRE TO REPEAT THE ACTION AND EVENTUALLY THE REPETITION WILL FORM A NEW HABIT (E.G. A WALK CAN BOOST MOOD, REFRESH AND REFOCUS).

YOU CAN'T EAT AN ELEPHANT IN ONE BITE

It's easy to fall into the trap of wanting to make huge changes in your life but I've been there and can tell you that it's unsustainable and can leave you feeling worse than when you started. As the saying goes: 'You can't eat an elephant in one bite.' Start small and make it so easy you can't say no. Decide what you want this new habit to be and then ask yourself, 'What can I do to make this habit so easy that I can't say no?' **In the beginning it's not about how well you do something, it's about starting and having realistic intentions.** Once the behaviour becomes consistent, you can build up to the level you want to achieve.

REMEMBER TO ENJOY IT!

Sixty-six days is a long time to do something you don't enjoy and you're more likely to fail in the first week if you dislike the activity. If you really enjoy eating food, then cutting back or cutting out certain foods will probably be difficult for you. Instead, it might help to think of how and when you eat food. Is it late at night? Is it around a table or in front of the TV? Perhaps you can start changing those aspects. If you don't like spinning but enjoy group classes, investigate other classes at your local gym. If you hate the gym, the local park might be the place to start. You don't have to run a 10K tomorrow if you sign up for one in six months; the point is to commit and show up, even if you only run for five minutes initially.

MINDSET TOOLKIT

When I was training for the Olympics I would journal everything, from races and times to my eating habits and inspirational quotes. This proved a really useful tool when I was feeling low; the ability to recount those positive moments – affirmations, the images of stadiums where I had run and photos of me crossing the finish line – was powerful. Whether it's a photo of a loved one or a positive quote on your fridge door, we all need a 'dangling carrot' to help us through the tough days. You don't have to be an elite athlete to benefit from the following techniques.

1

AFFIRMATIONS

Whether we're conscious of it or not, all of our self-talk is a stream of affirmations. Some work well for us, others don't. Paying attention to them allows us to recognise the negative and try to create a positive pattern. To put it simply, think happy thoughts.

2

VISUALISATION

There's a reason why the saying 'you have to see it to believe it' exists. If you've ever fantasised about winning that promotion, nailing that presentation, writing that book or completing that marathon, chances are you've already tapped into the visualisation tool. When we imagine our desired outcome, we begin to see the possibility of achieving it and the means to do so.

3

SELF-TALK

Negative self-talk can be paralysing. Take a moment to write down some of the negative and destructive messages you tell yourself. Then counteract those messages with positive truths in your life. The language we use directly relates to the state of our minds. Words like 'can't' and 'never' are disempowering. Sayings things like, 'I won't bother doing it as I'll just make a mistake' can be overwritten with, 'I can learn from my mistakes'.

4

PLANNING

The process of change starts with a good plan, one that works for you. Ensure you make time to create the right plan: it could be every Sunday evening or Monday morning for 20 minutes but it should be specific, realistic and achievable.

5

VISUAL REMINDERS

Before I won any athletic accolades I had a picture of an Olympic stadium as my screensaver, a beacon of where I could be if I put my mind to it. These days, it's an article I found many years ago about Roy Keane that is still stuck to my fridge, inspiring me every day. Whatever your hopes or dreams – getting fit, losing weight or starting a new business – a visual prompt can really help.

MONDAY

Spent quality time with Oscar.
Lucky to have a healthy family.
Got great feedback on last week's
presentation.

TUESDAY

Good group of friends.
Parents are fit and healthy.

WEDNESDAY

Lucky to be able to go on a
summer holiday.

THURSDAY

....
....
....
....
....

MAKING GRATITUDE A MINDSET

Many of us spend our time looking to the future for what's next or wishing for something we want. Nobody knows this better than an Olympic athlete, always striving to better their time or their competition, the focus always on their performance. And, while the spirit of competition is often what gets us over the line, an attitude of gratitude can enhance our character, which, in turn, improves performance. It may sound like a bit of a hippy ideal, but it is grounded in firm science. Studies have concluded that gratitude can have profound and positive effects on our mood and overall health.

Psychologist Martin Seligman, one of the pioneers of the 'positive psychology' movement, looked at six therapeutic interventions, and discovered that the practice of gratitude had the biggest short-term effect. **Participants who practised keeping a gratitude journal for a week enjoyed a huge increase in happiness scores and a lowering of depression levels.** The practice of writing a gratitude journal was an integral part of my athletic training programme; steering my mind towards gratitude, it turns out, made me a better and happier athlete and person. I would spend a few minutes before bed making a list of the things that had gone well for me that day, and the things for which I was grateful. It's amazing how powerful that exercise is for redirecting your thought patterns; by the time you're finished it's pretty hard not to feel good. Keep a pen and paper or diary/journal on your bedside table so that it's always at hand before you go to sleep.

The point is to write down at least three things you are grateful for every day. It could be as simple as starting with the fact that you have your sight or the roof over your head, your evening meal or the coffee you got to enjoy with an old friend. Instead of focusing on the guy who cut you off in traffic, focus on the one who yielded to you. Our tendency as humans is to focus on the negative, and writing down things we are grateful for rewires our thought patterns and motivates us to work harder or be more thoughtful to others.

BUILDING RESILIENCE

Why is it that some people bounce back from trauma better than others? Where does resilience come from? And why don't more of us have it? I believe that resilience – the capacity to endure stress and bounce back – is a skill we can learn and cultivate through adjusting our thinking and behaviour.

A long-term study of 99 Harvard men by psychiatrist George Vaillant found that the way they viewed negative life events (as fixed and unchangeable versus subject to growth) predicted their physical health. According to the study, resilience is linked to lower rates of depression and a longer life. Resilient people are characterised by an ability to experience negative and positive emotions. They may endure hardships but they are also able to find value in challenging moments. The men with good defence mechanisms were three times more likely to flourish later in life. Further evidence suggested that many of the individuals studied could write or rewrite their own life scripts, disproving F. Scott Fitzgerald's maxim that there are no second acts in our lives.

I'd like to think that I am living my second act thanks to resilience. We've all been tested and sometimes you wonder whether you're capable of bouncing back. I'm living proof that you can, but you have to put the effort in.

Improve your mindset in ten minutes:

1. **BREATHE**
TAKE A MOMENT AND BREATHE SLOWLY. REPEAT FOR FOUR OR FIVE BREATHS.

2. **GRATITUDE LIST**
MAKE A LIST OF FIVE THINGS YOU ARE GRATEFUL FOR TODAY.

3. **SET YOUR INTENTION FOR THE DAY**
HAVE CLEAR, REALISTIC INTENTIONS.

4. **LOOK BACK OR REMIND YOURSELF OF PAST ACHIEVEMENTS**
RECOUNT PAST SUCCESSES AND USE THEM TO STEER YOUR HEAD IN THE RIGHT DIRECTION.

5. **TAKE A FEW MINUTES OF 'ME' TIME**
MEDITATE, TAKE A BATH, GO FOR A WALK OR LISTEN TO YOUR FAVOURITE MUSIC OR PODCAST.

1
THINK POSITIVE

Sometimes this is harder than it sounds; it may come down to the mantra 'fake it till you make it' and the ability to be at least hopeful and challenge your self-talk. Be willing to try new things and allow yourself to make mistakes.

2
SELF-CARE

Make time for activities you enjoy and also time to recharge, whether that's a walk, reading a good book or catching up with friends. And ensure that you are getting enough sleep.

3
ESTABLISH INTENTIONS OR GOALS

Purpose helps focus and gives meaning to your life's activities. Plan ahead and focus on the process.

4
REFRAME THE SITUATION

Seeing the upside might involve looking at the situation a little differently. Instead of looking at the negative in the situation, try looking at the opportunities and what you can learn from it.

5
REMINDERS

Remind yourself of your successes and be grateful for what you have daily: your health, wealth, family, friends.

6
ENGAGEMENT

Try to be present and engage with family, friends and work colleagues – this will strengthen your relationships and make them more rewarding.

2. MOVEMENT

'Change happens through
movement, and movement heals'
JOSEPH PILATES

One moment that stands out in my road to recovery in my mental state is the day I left the house to do my first bit of exercise in over a year. It was a Monday morning and my wife Charlotte had been encouraging me for months to join her at a kettlebell class. Why would I want to do that, I thought. Why would I pay €10 for someone to tell me what I already know? I'm the athlete here! I'd be much better off staying away from those group classes and doing it myself. Except I didn't do it myself – I just sat at home nursing my ego instead.

That Monday I decided to push past my comfort zone and I joined the class. When I walked in, everyone stared. I'll admit I was uncomfortable and spent the first ten minutes wondering how I could escape. But then I started to forget 'the audience' and engage with the class, a pattern I was used to from my racing days. By the end I had signed up for the following week.

Most of us can relate to the feeling of being judged; to me it was often a 'handicap' to my motivation. Every Saturday I join the VHI Park Run in Marlay Park, Dublin and every week someone will ask me what time I ran, occasionally telling me they thought I would have 'run it faster'. Initially this was enough to deter me from going. My position was always one of defence, tripping over myself to explain that a park run is different from the 400m sprint. Now I'm honest and tell them I haven't run in a while and there's always room for improvement. In simple terms, I've accepted where I am. The competition is really only with myself, plus the reward I get post-run or exercise far outweighs the pain of deliberation or the guilt that comes with doing nothing.

As humans we are wired to be active but a lot of us avoid exercise because we believe it's too difficult, time-consuming, painful or exhausting or that we just aren't cut out for it. Maybe you don't like it or maybe you're afraid or embarrassed about not knowing what to do in a gym or being the 'worst' in a class. **Whatever the excuse, it's usually just that, an excuse with too much power.**

HOW MUCH EXERCISE DO WE REALLY NEED?

Most of us have a magic number we believe we should hit in order to reach our exercise goal. **The national guideline for recommended physical activity is 5 x 30 minutes a week**, and I think that's a sound goal to aim for. It may not seem like much for the more active among us, but for others it's plain scary. It's really the idea of the commitment that scares some people – committing to moving your body five out of seven days a week. This fear often ends up 'sabotaging' a routine before it's even got off the ground.

Facing this fear head-on is the key. Start off with doing something every second day and start small, even as small as five minutes. If the goal is achievable it will help form the habit. The important thing is you get your heart rate up and build a routine that combines a mix of mobility, cardio and strength exercises – I will talk about this a bit more later in the chapter.

BUILDING A PERSONAL FITNESS PLAN

Champions are not born, they are made. The same applies to anything in life and it starts with commitment. Let's talk about your own fitness plan.

* **BE HONEST WITH YOURSELF**
  What are the real reasons your current way of doing things isn't working? What's stopping you? Perhaps you need some additional support such as counselling to help with anxiety or depression, or a 'training buddy' to exercise with. Maybe you just find it boring, in which case it's time to change the format. You might think you don't have time, but there is nearly always a way. The point is to try to break down the excuses and push through.

The next step is to build the plan. It's not enough to talk (or write) about what you're going to do – you need something concrete to work from, involving days, times, specific exercises, quantities, etc. Your list tells you *why* you are doing this but *how many days a week* can you realistically fit into your life and at what times? What are you actually going to do?

GET A NOTEBOOK AND WRITE DOWN THE ANSWERS TO THE FOLLOWING QUESTIONS:

1
WHY ARE YOU DOING IT?

E.g. Weight loss, better fitness, improved flexibility, overall health, to meet people through exercise.

2
WHAT DO YOU WANT TO ACHIEVE?

E.g. Lose a stone, run 5K, take up tennis, learn how to play golf, improve your muscle tone.

3
ARE YOU MAXIMISING YOUR POTENTIAL?

E.g. Are you playing to your strengths and weaknesses? Maybe you already run regularly but don't do any resistance exercises, or you go to a class but don't feel you're getting much out of it. Think about the things you are already doing well and the things you could improve.

4
HOW DO YOU FEEL AFTER EXERCISING?

E.g. Energised, proud, positive.

LET THESE BE THE MOTIVATORS FOR STICKING WITH THE PLAN.

Before you hit the gym make a plan of five exercises you're going to do, the equipment you want to use (if applicable) and the body parts you want to target. There's no point trying to squeeze something in at the end of the day when you're exhausted as you're more likely to skip it and thus feel worse. The idea is that you want to attain long-term consistency.

- **BE REALISTIC.** What else is going on in your life? Your programme needs to work with your lifestyle, so if you have children, a demanding job or other responsibilities you really need to work out where your new plan will fit in. If you are over-ambitious you are setting yourself up for disappointment, so don't set unrealistic goals.

- **START WITH WHAT FEELS GOOD.** There's a bit of a myth about running in that it seems to be inextricably linked with getting fit. It's often the first exercise people think of when embarking on a fitness regime only to discover they hate it! Maybe you'd enjoy a team sport or something you did when you were younger – it helps to consider the activities from which you get pleasure and work them into your routine. The chances are if you enjoyed it at school, you're likely to enjoy it now.

- **START SMALL.** When you're starting out, there's nothing like the idea of an hour-long exercise class to put you off. Doing something that goes on too long is often a stumbling block. Rein it back to five or ten minutes and build it up. Go for a walk if that seems more achievable.

- **BE ACCOUNTABLE.** Nobody wants to be the new person in the classroom with no one to play with. Sometimes we need to rely on a training buddy to stay motivated. It's very likely you know someone who is also interested in getting fit, running a 10K or joining the gym. Join forces, and keep on top of each other to keep going – there's nothing like accountability to keep you motivated.

- **CONSIDER YOUR ENVIRONMENT.** When I was training in the UK I was surrounded by like-minded people who shared the same interests and objectives. This was integral when it came to living and training. Who are the people around you? Do they share the same interests when it comes to exercising? If there is someone who is constantly putting you down or mocking your efforts to become fitter, it might be time to take a step back and rethink your environment.

- **MANAGE YOUR EXPECTATIONS.** It's important to remember that getting fit and healthy isn't your full-time career, so allow for plenty of 'bad' days when

you may not hit your target or manage to fit in any exercise. I always loved the quote by humanitarian Rudy Rasmus, 'expectations are premeditated resentments' – it reminds us of the toxic nature of expectations and how they can breed contempt. If we have unrealistic expectations of ourselves that aren't met then we potentially develop contempt for ourselves. Loosen the rope, allow yourself some flexibility and don't allow the regime to control everything. It may be helpful to revisit the wheel of life technique (p.17) to ensure there is good balance between the key areas of your life.

- **RE-EVALUATE.** If you don't think something is worth doing, stop and re-evaluate. It could involve changing a few small things such as when you eat, the type of gym class you attend or when you do your run – re-evaluating your 'programme' at the end of every week can help sustain the long-term goal.

- **DEVELOP ACCEPTANCE.** One of the catalysts to my improved health was accepting I wasn't the athlete I once was. I stopped trying to replicate past achievements when I admitted that I'm not a professional athlete anymore. That applies to life beyond the track, too. I no longer count calories or adhere to a strict food routine. I eat the cake! Accept where you are in your life today

and realise that although you're not going to become an elite athlete or even run a marathon, you can still improve your fitness and wellbeing hugely with small steps.

MOBILITY, STRENGTH AND CARDIO

Mixing up your training is crucial to get the most from your exercise programme and see the best results. Whatever form of exercise you embark upon, you need to incorporate **mobility, cardio** and **strength** into your regime. Beware of approaching exercise as just another box to be ticked – it's not enough to just turn up at the gym; you need to push yourself a bit or raise your heart rate to reap the rewards.

MOBILITY

In simple terms, mobility means having a good range of motion. As we get older, our joints get stiffer and our bodies slow down so mobility becomes a real investment. Have you ever thought about how long you spend sitting down every day? Chances are it's more than you think. As soon as you get out of a chair your blood sugar improves, it promotes blood flow recovery and reduces chances of injury. Being more mobile could be as simple as skipping the bus and walking or cycling to work, taking the stairs instead of the lift, taking a walk around the block at lunchtime or standing while talking on the phone. You don't have to address the whole body; start with something accessible and that you can manage to do every day without strenuous effort. You can then build on it once you feel ready.

EXAMPLES OF MOBILITY EXERCISES

ANYTHING THAT GETS YOU UP AND MOVING AND ALLOWS FOR A RANGE OF MOTION SUCH AS WALKING, STRETCHING, STAIR CLIMBING. IT ALSO INCLUDES DISCIPLINES SUCH AS YOGA, TAI CHI AND PILATES.

STRENGTH

Once you reach the age of 35 you start losing 1 per cent of your strength every year. Muscle mass and strength depletes unless we work to maintain it. A strength-based exercise involves resistance or moving a force, whether that's your body weight or a gym weight. The benefits of doing weight-bearing exercises are huge. They can help promote lean muscle mass, improve bone health and overall strength, prevent injury and, if you're a runner, improve your running technique. It's not all about bulk or size either; regular strength training will help tone, sculpt and boost muscle definition.

EXAMPLES OF STRENGTH-BASED EXERCISES

LIFTING WEIGHTS OR YOUR OWN BODY WEIGHT SUCH AS SQUATS, LUNGES, PULL-UPS AND PUSH-UPS.

CARDIO

Your heart and lungs are both muscles that need to be worked just like any other muscle in your body. Lifting 100kg in weights is all very well, but if you're not getting your heart rate up (i.e. making it beat faster than normal), you're not working that muscle. Cardio exercises are traditionally designed to use fat as fuel and to increase your lung capacity and endurance stamina, and get your heart rate up.

EXAMPLES OF CARDIO EXERCISES

ANYTHING OVER THREE MINUTES THAT WORKS YOUR HEART AND LUNGS SUCH AS SPINNING, CYCLING, RUNNING, ROWING, THE STEP MACHINE, AEROBIC CLASSES, JUMPING JACKS AND BURPEES.

Take the talk test – if you can talk comfortably during exercise then you're not working hard enough! If you reach a point where you've stagnated, it's time to change it up or push yourself harder. The talk test relates to any form of exercise, so don't be afraid to get that heart going and leave the chinwag to the end.

RESTING HEART RATE

When I was training full-time we used heart rate to monitor our overall health. It was important to monitor our resting heart rate (i.e. how fast the heart is beating when you're not doing any exercise) in order to spot any sudden increase, which could suggest injury or illness. If it was five beats higher than normal, it indicated a change in equilibrium that usually meant you were run down or fighting a bug. If it was 10 beats higher, you weren't training. The fitter you are the lower it will be.

I recently got back into running by going for a regular long run. I felt very unfit to begin with and decided I needed to build my cardio by pounding some pavement. After a few runs I was unsure if I was working hard enough; yes, I was out of breath when I finished but I didn't really know if I was running fast enough or slow enough to get maximum effort. I decided to focus on my heart rate and use it to guide me when out on the road.

The best way of monitoring your heart rate is by taking your pulse over a minute first thing in the morning, literally when you wake up, while you are 'rested'. By doing this over a course of time you will begin to find out what your average resting heart rate or BPM (beats per minute) is. This figure becomes your base line, and if you find a day when your resting heart rate is five or 10 beats higher, it could suggest that you are a little under the weather and maybe a rest day is best.

Activities that can provoke change in resting heart rate include physical exercise, quality of sleep, anxiety, stress and illness. From a training point of view your heart can tell you how hard you are working and there are certain zones to aim for.

CALCULATING YOUR RESTING HEART RATE

We all have a personal resting heart rate and a maximum heart rate (MHR). And between these values are different heart rate zones that correspond to training intensity and training benefit.

First, you need to find your resting heart rate.

1. **FIND YOUR PULSE**
   WITH YOUR FINGERS (NOT YOUR THUMB) WHILE LYING DOWN.

2. **COUNT YOUR PULSE**
   FOR 15 SECONDS AND MULTIPLY BY FOUR.

3. **RECORD YOUR HEART RATE**
   ONCE A DAY FOR FIVE DAYS.

4. **ADD THE FIVE RESTING HEART RATES**
   TOGETHER AND DIVIDE BY FIVE TO FIND YOUR AVERAGE RESTING HEART RATE.

TYPE OF EXERCISE	DURATION	INTENSITY LEVEL
VERY HIGH ANAEROBIC 90–100% MHR (MAXIMUM HEART RATE)	1–5 MIN	**MAXIMUM INTENSITY** – short sprints or bursts of activity. Good for athletic conditioning. High-intensity interval workouts and interval running are great examples of building maximum workouts into your training.
HIGH AEROBIC 80–90% MHR	2–10 MIN	**MODERATE INTENSITY** – improves endurance. Your body will get better at using carbohydrates for energy and you'll be able to withstand higher levels of lactic acid in your blood for longer. Examples include power walking, running, spinning, circuits. Good for building endurance, cardiovascular health.
MEDIUM WEIGHT LOSS 60–80% MHR	10–20 MIN	**MEDIUM INTENSITY** – effective for improving the efficiency of blood circulation in the heart and skeletal muscles. Examples include brisk walking, jogging, cycling. Good for burning fat, increasing endurance and general heart health.
LIGHT 50–60% MHR	20–60 MIN	**LIGHT INTENSITY** – improves your general endurance: your body will get better at oxidising (burning) fat and your muscular fitness will increase. Examples include slow jog, walk, new exercises. Good for beginners and overall health.

Now find your maximum heart rate (MHR) by subtracting your age from 220. For example, for a forty-year-old, subtract 40 to get 180. This gives you a figure that is the number of beats per minute of your heart when working at its maximum effort.

Exercise takes place at varying levels of intensity, which affects heart rate.

Anaerobic (without oxygen) exercise is high-intensity activity that causes you to be quickly out of breath, like sprinting or lifting a heavy weight.

Aerobic (with oxygen) is a steady-state endurance activity. If you're working out in an aerobic range you should feel like you can keep moving for a longer duration.

Below that, there is medium intensity, which is good for weight loss, and light intensity, which improves endurance.

Each of these types of exercise is beneficial for different reasons, and you can see the target heart rate ranges on the previous page.

HIGH-INTENSITY INTERVAL TRAINING

There's a misconception that for optimum fitness you have to work out for a long period of time, but in fact, studies show that high-intensity interval training (popularly known as HIIT), is the ideal type of workout. Studies done by Dr Niels Volaard, a lecturer in health and science at the University of Stirling, showed that when people complete fewer sprint repetitions, it may even produce *better* cardiorespiratory results than long workouts. In his opinion, lack of time is frequently used as one of the main barriers to people becoming or staying physically active. High-intensity workouts allow people to get the maximum health benefits while working out for a shorter time.

HIIT involves repetitions of short bursts of intense, maximum-effort exercise for approximately 30–60 seconds followed by equal periods of rest. Think 30 seconds to a minute of cycling or sprinting followed by a minute or two of walking or slow pedalling and repeating this circuit for 10 minutes. The theory is that by working out at your maximum level of exertion, you burn more calories in a short space of time. In addition, HIIT speeds up your metabolism for up to 24 hours after working out, which means you're burning calories after you've finished exercising.

Some more benefits are:

* **Helps burn fat**
* **Builds lean muscle mass**
* **No equipment or gym necessary**
* **Increases metabolism**
* **Slows the ageing process**
* **Improves oxygen consumption**
* **Reduces heart rate, blood pressure and blood sugar.**

Note: HIIT is probably not a great starting point if you haven't exercised for a while. You will need to start more gently and build up to it.

CIRCUIT TRAINING

An ideal circuit combines mobility, cardio and strength in one set. A **set** is the number of reps you perform and a **rep** denotes the repetition of a movement or exercise.

Circuits are a way of combining different elements of exercise into one training session. I've given some sample circuits for you to try at the end of this chapter.

TRAINING FOR WEIGHT LOSS

Wanting to lose weight and finding the motivation to do so are very different things. Most people who want to lose weight usually have a figure of their ideal weight in their heads. How they get there is often the tricky bit. The fact is, losing weight is not just about calorie restriction and getting active; it starts with your state of mind. Losing weight is a massive mental challenge that requires commitment, stamina and rational thought.

In Chapter 1 I spoke about finding your 'why'. First, you need to ask yourself *why* you want to lose weight and then mentally commit to the process. Changing one meal or one workout isn't going to make you thinner or overweight; you need to put a bit of time in, and take a holistic approach to losing weight. Realise that rest and mental attitude are just as important in the weight-loss process as diet and exercise.

Looking at your energy intake is a good starting point when you want to lose weight. **Are you consuming more calories than you're burning?** Another thing to consider if you're hitting the gym regularly is the fact that building muscle might mean losing fat but may also mean gaining a few pounds on the scales. Those extra digits you see with frustration on the display could be new muscle mass!

FIVE QUICK TIPS TO
A BETTER FITNESS PLAN

1
ALTERNATE
YOUR EXERCISES

From upper to lower body,
arms, legs, etc.

2
KEEP IT
FUNCTIONAL

Pushing, pulling, walking, bending
– everyday tasks that you can
incorporate no matter where
you are.

3
KEEP IT
REALISTIC

What can you do and when?

4
ALLOW FOR SHORT
RECOVERY TIMES

30 seconds in between
short bursts of
exercising.

5
CONSIDER QUICK
CIRCUIT SESSIONS

Try cardio circuit (HIIT) for
time efficiency and high
intensity.

Your approach to weight loss should also be sustainable. If you change your lifestyle too quickly, too radically, it's not going to last. Building slow lifestyle changes will reap better rewards. Speaking of rewards, it's important to allow yourself non-food rewards when you've reached some of your mini-goals. There's no point ruining all that effort with a binge on a takeaway and a few drinks – the idea is to 'treat' yourself but not necessarily undo all your hard work. Non-food treats could include a massage, some new sports gear or a book you've been wanting to read.

FIVE EXERCISES TO PROMOTE WEIGHT LOSS

1. **SHORT SPRINTS**
   10-SECOND SPRINT, 20-SECOND SLOW RECOVERY JOG; 10 SETS

2. **SQUATS, WEIGHTS**
   FIVE SETS OF 10 REPETITIONS

3. **LUNGES**
   FIVE SETS OF 10 REPETITIONS

4. **DIPS**
   FIVE SETS OF 10 REPETITIONS

5. **PUSH-UPS**
   FIVE SETS OF 10 REPETITIONS

CHANGING IT UP

Our bodies are amazing machines that will adapt to changes we make, which is why alternating our routine is important, especially for weight loss. Walking and/or jogging will increase your cardio and overall endurance, and this can be a good way to start losing weight, but if this is *all* you are doing, eventually you will reach a plateau and any changes will be minimal.

The body becomes desensitised to exercise and stagnates if we are in a repetitive cycle, and it can lead to boredom and a lack of motivation. Changing up your routine every three weeks keeps it challenging, interesting and stimulates both the body and the mind. When I was training full-time we worked off four-week **periodised plans** with three heavy training weeks followed by one week of recovery. The sessions in the next four-week plan would be different, which forced me to work hard to adapt. 'Periodisation' simply means planning physical training in cycles with different exercises/levels of intensity to avoid staleness or plateauing.

It's so important at any level to keep exercise exciting and challenging as this will maintain motivation and help you reach your goals.

Changing things up will boost your metabolism as the body adapts to the new workload, while helping to work on toning other areas of your body, e.g. legs, arms, etc. A study conducted at the Human Performance Laboratory at Ball State University in Indiana has shown that a periodised strength-training programme can produce better results than a non-periodised programme:

For effective weight loss, try to include some conditioning exercises into your daily routine. For example, instead of running most days of the week, include some weight-bearing exercises such as squats, lunges, push-ups and crunches. Do these in sets, for example 10 repetitions of each exercise repeated three times. After a few weeks, increase the sets or even change the type of exercise. Mixing it up like this will give you visible results (i.e. tone and weight loss) in a relatively small amount of time, complement your cardio work and help improve your overall fitness.

FIVE SIMPLE WAYS TO CHANGE YOUR TRAINING

1. **CHANGE THE NUMBER** OF REPETITIONS PER SET, OR THE NUMBER OF SETS OF EACH EXERCISE.

2. **CHANGE THE AMOUNT** OF RESISTANCE USED.

3. **CHANGE THE REST** PERIOD BETWEEN SETS, EXERCISES OR TRAINING SESSIONS.

4. **CHANGE THE ORDER** OF THE EXERCISES, OR THE TYPES OF EXERCISES.

5. **CHANGE THE SPEED** AT WHICH YOU COMPLETE EACH EXERCISE

GET OUTSIDE!

There is a lot you can do with your body that doesn't involve high-impact gym sessions. Look outside – the world is your gym and it's free! Exercise can run the risk of becoming a chore, something that's at the end of your to-do list, especially if you have to get in your car to drive to the gym. This goes back to the all-important mindset of fitness – seeing ways to incorporate it into your daily life takes the pressure off. What could be easier than putting your runners on and heading out the door for a quick run or even a brisk walk?

You can exercise just about anywhere: the house, garden, local park or football pitch. An added benefit of getting outside is the dose of nature (and sunlight if you're lucky), considered to be hugely beneficial to your health. Just five minutes of 'green' exercise – physical activity in the presence of nature – can benefit mental health and wellbeing. Studies have found that physical activity in a natural environment promoted feelings of revital-isation and encouragement and reduced tension, anger, confusion and depression. Good news for those who find the gym environment off-putting.

MINI WORKOUTS

There are some basic body weight exercises that can be combined in many different ways to give you different types of workouts depending on how long you have and where you are. The great thing about these exercises is that you can do them almost anywhere – at home, in the park or in the gym. Before you get started, take a bit of time to make sure you have got the hang of doing each exercise correctly.

The exercises on the next few pagwes combine to work all the key parts of your body – legs, upper body, cardio and core.

LEGS

1. SQUATS

2. LUNGES

3. BRIDGES

UPPER BODY

4. PUSH-UPS

5. TRICEP DIP

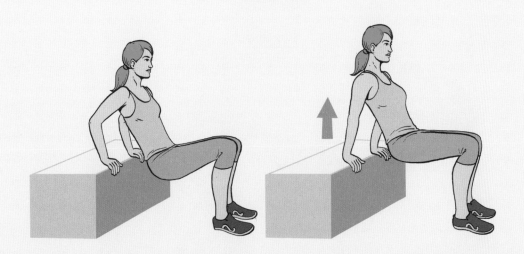

CARDIO

6. JUMPING JACKS

7. BURPEES

CORE

8. PLANK

9. ABDOMINAL CRUNCHES

10. BACK RAISES

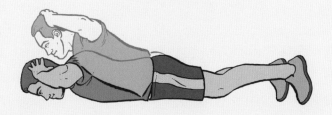

HOME WORKOUT

10 MINUTES - PLAN A

*Do each exercise for 40 seconds;
rest for 20 seconds in between each.*

JUMPING JACKS
SQUATS
PUSH-UPS
PLANK
BURPEES
LUNGES
TRICEP DIPS
BACK RAISES
CRUNCHES
JUMPING JACKS

10 MINUTES - PLAN B

*Repeat
circuit 3 times.*

30 JUMPING JACKS
15 PUSH-UPS
PLANK – 30 seconds
10 BURPEES
20 LUNGES
30 JUMPING JACKS
BRIDGE – 30 seconds

15 MINUTES

*Complete 3 rounds of the following,
20 seconds per exercise, and
10 seconds off.*

JUMPING JACKS
SQUATS
PUSH-UPS
PLANK
BURPEES
LUNGES
TRICEP DIPS
BACK RAISES
CRUNCHES
JUMPING JACKS

20 MINUTES

*Complete 4 rounds of the following,
20 seconds per exercise,
and 10 seconds off.*

JUMPING JACKS
SQUATS
PUSH-UPS
PLANK
BURPEES
LUNGES
TRICEP DIPS
BACK RAISES
CRUNCHES
JUMPING JACKS

PITCH WORKOUT

10 MINUTE - OPTION A

*Using the length of a football pitch
with an exercise at each end.
Repeat circuit twice.*

RUN THE LENGTH
12 PUSH–UPS
RUN THE LENGTH
10 LUNGES – each leg
RUN THE LENGTH
12 SQUATS
RUN THE LENGTH
PLANK 30 SECONDS
RUN THE LENGTH

10 MINUTE - OPTION B

*Using the length and width of
a football pitch with an exercise at
opposite corners.*

RUN THE LENGTH, WALK THE WIDTH
10 LUNGES - alternate legs
RUN THE LENGTH, WALK THE WIDTH
10 PUSH-UPS
RUN THE LENGTH, WALK THE WIDTH
10 SQUATS
RUN THE LENGTH, WALK THE WIDTH
10 BRIDGES
RUN THE LENGTH, WALK THE WIDTH
10 JUMPING JACKS
RUN THE LENGTH, WALK THE WIDTH
10 BURPEES

OUTDOOR WORKOUT

15 MINUTES - OPTION A

Running workout along with body weight exercises.

JOG – 20 seconds
SPRINT – 20 seconds
WALK – 20 seconds

Repeat the above 4 times, rest for 1 minute and do the following:

30 SQUATS
30 PUSH-UPS
30 BRIDGES
30 LUNGES
30 BACK RAISES

Rest for 1 minute and finish off with running, again 4 sets:

JOG – 20 seconds
SPRINT – 20 seconds
WALK – 20 seconds

20 MINUTES - OPTION A

Take a 30-second break between rounds, repeat 4 times.

SPRINT – 45 seconds, 15 seconds off
10 PUSH-UPS
20 SQUATS
15 BACK RAISES
PLANK – 30 seconds
20 LUNGES – alternate legs
SPRINT – 45 seconds, 15 seconds off

15 MINUTES - OPTION B

Running workout along with body weight exercises. Repeat 3 rounds of:

SPRINT – 40 seconds, 20 seconds off
PUSH-UPS – 40 seconds, 20 seconds off
CRUNCHES – 40 seconds, 20 seconds off
LUNGES – alternate legs 40 seconds, 20 seconds off
PLANK – 40 seconds, 20 seconds off

20 MINUTES - OPTION B

ON THE MINUTE EVERY MINUTE:

You have a full minute to complete these exercises. Use whatever time you have left over as your break. Rest for 1 minute between each set. Do circuit 4 times.

20 SQUATS
15 BURPEES
20 LUNGES – ALTERNATE LEGS
1 SPRINT OF THE PITCH – length
20 CRUNCHES
30 PUSH-UPS
15 BRIDGES
SPRINT – 45 seconds, 15 seconds off

OUTDOOR WORKOUT RUNNING

There are so many benefits to taking up running – not least the fact that all you need is some basic running gear and you're ready to go. Once you step out of the door of your house you're on the way. A Couch to 5K programme is a great way to get started – there are lots available to download but they all follow more or less the same concept:

1. **CHOOSE A GOAL**
   MAYBE YOU JUST WANT TO GET STARTED, OR YOU MIGHT WANT TO RUN A MARATHON, IT'S UP TO YOU. BUT START SMALL AND BUILD UP GRADUALLY.

2. **GET ORGANISED**
   PICK THE TIMES DURING THE WEEK THAT YOU WILL RUN AND MAKE SURE THEY ARE IN YOUR DIARY. AIM TO BUILD UP TO THREE SESSIONS OVER THE WEEK.

3. **SORT YOUR GEAR**
   INVEST IN THE CORRECT RUNNING SHOES FOR YOUR FEET, COMFORTABLE CLOTHES. DOWNLOAD A TRACKING APP.

4. **DON'T FORGET TO WARM UP**
   USE LIGHT JOGGING AND SOME FUNCTIONAL MOVEMENTS SUCH AS LUNGES, SQUATS AND STRIDES.

5. **JOIN A RUNNING GROUP**
   IT'S GREAT TO KEEP IT SOCIAL AND HAVE PEOPLE OF A SIMILAR LEVEL AROUND YOU. ALL YOU HAVE TO DO IS TURN UP AND RUN.

6. **WATCH OUT FOR INJURIES**
   LISTEN TO YOUR BODY AND DON'T BE AFRAID TO PULL BACK IF SORENESS ARISES. REST IS AS IMPORTANT AS TRAINING.

7. **CHANGE IT UP**
   VARY YOUR ROUTE AND YOUR TRAINING SESSION.

For example, if you can do three training sessions over the course of a week, start with a steady-paced long run. When starting out, no matter your goal, you're aiming to build up to a long, steady run, which is great for weight management and building cardiovascular fitness.

Your second session would be interval-based – a period of activity followed by a period of rest. This type of session is great to build fitness in a time-efficient manner. Intervals can be time-based or distance-based and the idea is to run each repetition at a fast pace. An example of an interval session could be 5 x 1 minute with 1 minute recovery in between. Altering the session is easily done by changing the time, the number of reps, the recovery time or the environment.

The final session could be a tempo run. This is a run shorter in duration than a long run but at a higher speed, but not as fast as the speed of your interval repetitions. This is a great session for building speed endurance, weight management and overall fitness.

HOW TO MEASURE YOUR PROGRESS

Seeing progress after a few weeks of exercise can be a great motivator to keep going. Progress can be measured in different ways and will be personal to you depending on your goals. Here are some examples.

* **Track your weight on a weekly basis.**
* **Exercises such as running are weight-bearing, so calves, bum and legs will begin to tone. Keep a measurement of these.**
* **Keep an eye on the times and the distances you are running, amounts you are exercising or reps you are achieving.**

* **Are you enjoying it? If not, don't beat yourself up, maybe a certain exercise isn't your thing. But there is another activity out there that you *will* enjoy, so give everything a go!**

3. REST

'If you get tired, learn to rest,

not to quit.'

BANSKY

More than **60** years ago, English-American poet W.H. Auden wrote a Pulitzer Prize-winning poem called 'The Age of Anxiety' – a reflection of the human condition in 1940s New York. The phrase has since been used to characterise the consciousness of various moments in history. Never has it been more applicable than right now when our lives have become hijacked by the perils of modern living.

In my opinion, we have never been more anxious, stressed, overwhelmed or tired. Many people I know are busy and exhausted by the breakneck pace of life. Add to that the information overload we are bombarded with daily, and it's no wonder we're stressed. If we are in the 'Age of Anxiety', then we are also in the 'Age of Distraction' with new research by British psychologists showing that around one-third of our waking hours is spent using technology, with phones being used on average five times an hour, every waking hour.

It's been proven that technology use can impair attention and productivity, increase stress levels and reduce sleep quality. It has also extended office hours long past the traditional nine-to-five parameters. There's no off-switch to stop work-related emails and texts being sent to our smart-phones. The new technological age that is supposed to bring us great freedom by introducing more flexibility is, in turn, slowly destroying us.

Work demands, financial strain, high expectations and family life also contribute to elevated stress levels. We feel anxious and guilty when we aren't working and busyness has become a sort of existential reassurance. Even children are busy these days, with their weekdays and weekends scheduled down to the half-hour with extracurricular activities.

One thing that has not changed with all this 'progress', however, is the basic human need for sleep. According to the World Health Organisation (WHO) we are experiencing a sleep deficit epidemic, with two-thirds of adults in developed nations not getting the recommended eight hours of sleep a night. In 1942, less than 8 per cent of the British population was trying to survive on only six hours sleep a night; in 2017, almost one in two people were. Many might put a good night's sleep low on their list of what is the most important thing for good health – a physiological function that is optional – but the fact is that sleep is an active process that works to help repair the mind and body, as does good rest. It's also been proven to work against the development of diseases such as cancer, Alzheimer's and diabetes, and obesity.

I have to put my hand up at this point and admit that of the four pillars in this book, rest and recovery is the one I struggle with the most, yet consider to be the most important. My athletic training has conditioned me to move; I was built to keep going, but rest and recovery were also key components of my training. The body needs to have an adaptation phase so it can benefit from all the exercise.

I'm not the only one who struggles with getting adequate rest and recovery – many find the very idea of adding another thing to the to-do list, even if it is self-care, another burden and not as important as other things on that list.

STRESS

So what is stress? We can broadly define it as the body's response to any demand put on it, and not even the most mindful and chilled-out guru is completely immune to it. Scientists have known for years that elevated levels of the stress hormone cortisol interfere with our physical and mental wellbeing: millions of working days are lost to stress-related illnesses each year. A self-care report carried out in Ireland by Unilever found that 64 per cent of people surveyed claimed that stress was a constant part of their everyday lives.

A small amount of stress isn't bad for us; it can actually be a good motivator, priming us with helpful energy for various challenging events. Problems arise when we endure it for long periods of time. Cortisol is released by the adrenal glands in response to fear or stress as part of the fight-or-flight response, a survival mechanism enabling humans to react quickly to life-threatening situations. It goes back to when our ancient ancestors lived in real danger daily and actually needed the response to help them survive. Unfortunately, the body can overreact and trigger this same response to everyday, non-life-threatening situations such as work pressure, relationship troubles or bad traffic. Once the alarm to release cortisol is sounded, your body moves to action in that fight-or-flight mode. When there is no release of fight-or-flight, your body is left feeling under attack; cortisol levels build up in the blood, which in turn affect the body.

Our 'always-on' culture makes it difficult to switch off and find that space for ourselves, but this is the first step in combating stress and normalising our cortisol levels. Who has the time to 'commune' with themselves, though? How can you learn to make the time? Read on to find out ...

SCHEDULING IN YOURSELF

Make a conscious decision to give yourself some time every day. If you can't manage 30 minutes, try 15. If you can't manage 15, five minutes is better than nothing and for those minutes make sure there are no technology interruptions and that the time is for you and you alone.

* **MEDITATE**
(SEE PAGE 69 FOR TECHNIQUES). EVEN FIVE MINUTES OF MEDITATION WILL HAVE A POSITIVE IMPACT.

* **LISTEN TO YOUR FAVOURITE PODCAST OR MUSIC**
YOU COULD PLUG YOURSELF INTO YOUR SMARTPHONE AND TAKE A WALK AT THE SAME TIME.

* **HAVE A BATH**
USE YOUR FAVOURITE BATH OIL, LIGHT CANDLES, LOCK THE DOOR AND MAKE IT CLEAR YOU WANT AT LEAST 15 MINUTES WITH NO INTERRUPTIONS.

* **GO FOR A WALK IN NATURE**
BE MINDFUL, TAKING IN EVERYTHING YOU SEE AND HEAR, FROM BIRDS TO BUDS ON TREES AND LEAVES ON THE GROUND.

* **READ A BOOK**
SETTLE DOWN IN A COMFORTABLE CHAIR, WITH GOOD LIGHT, AND LOSE YOURSELF IN A BOOK.

* **PRACTISE YOGA**
THIS IS A WAY TO EXERCISE THAT ALSO FEEDS YOUR MIND AND AIDS RELAXATION WONDERFULLY.

TECHNOLOGY – SETTING BOUNDARIES

The dreaded T word. Don't get me wrong, I love technology. Modern gadgets make life easier. Where would we honestly be without them? Then again, how did we manage without them? Because we did – years ago if you wanted the news you'd buy a paper or switch on the television at a certain time. Now it's 24/7 and we're getting our dopamine 'high' from exposure to it. Dopamine is the pleasure neurotransmitter in the brain that relates to our bodies' reward systems. In Silicon Valley, dopamine is referred to as the 'secret sauce' that makes an app, game or social media platform 'sticky', or popular and profitable.

As humans we are wired to connect but by opening the door to technology we have closed the door on ourselves. Our always-on ethos has meant little or no time for reflection; there is always something out there 'robbing' us of ourselves.

Our downtime has become time spent on social media as opposed to getting outside or getting creative. Even walks in the park or dinners with friends are broadcast for all to see. We may all love technology but it can leave a trail of wreckage in its wake. It has accelerated the pace of our lives and shows no signs of abating. All the numbers confirm that we are addicted. According to studies, a typical smartphone user will touch their phone 2,617 times every day. That's a staggering statistic but when we think about it, reaching for our phone is often the first thing we do before we even get out of bed in the morning and looking at our phone is often the last thing we do before we go to sleep.

When I was struggling to motivate myself I found social media – the mechanism that promises inclusion – extremely isolating. I would spend hours on my phone comparing myself to other athletes only to be left feeling I wasn't fulfilling my potential. It had a direct effect on my confidence. I eventually detached myself from it by closing down my Facebook account. I still use it but I'm conscious of my interaction and how much time I spend on it.

In addition there is a growing health concern over exposure to blue light from TV, computer and smartphone screens. Until the advent of artificial lighting, the sun was the major source of brightness. Now we are basking in the 'blue light' from our technology, which, experts believe, throws the body's biological clock out of whack. Researchers at Harvard Medical School compared the effects of exposure to blue light and found that the light suppressed melatonin – which aids your natural sleep cycle – and shifted circadian rhythms (our internal 'clocks' that cycle between sleepiness and alertness).

The good news is that it's within our power to address our relationship, and make the right choices when it comes to technology. Ask yourself the following questions to find out where your boundaries are currently:

1. **ARE YOU SENDING WORK EMAILS** LATE AT NIGHT EXPECTING RESPONSES?

2. **DO YOU WORK** OVER THE WEEKEND?

3. **ARE YOU REACHING FOR YOUR PHONE** FOR NO APPARENT REASON BUT TO CHECK SOCIAL MEDIA AT REGULAR INTERVALS?

4. **DO YOU LOOK AT YOUR PHONE** REGULARLY WHEN YOU'RE OUT SOCIALISING WITH FRIENDS OR FAMILY?

5. **DO YOU OFTEN EAT** IN FRONT OF THE TELEVISION?

6. **IS YOUR INTERACTION WITH YOUR PHONE** AFFECTING CLOSE RELATION-SHIPS WITH YOUR PARTNER, FRIENDS OR CHILDREN?

7. **HOW OFTEN DO YOU SIT** AROUND THE TABLE FOR A FAMILY MEAL WITHOUT YOUR PHONE BESIDE YOU?

If you feel that the time has come for you to reduce your use of technology try some of the following tips.

TIPS FOR DIGITAL DETOXING

1. **REMOVE TELEVISIONS FROM YOUR BEDROOM.**

2. **BUY AN ALARM CLOCK** AND USE IT INSTEAD OF YOUR PHONE TO WAKE YOU UP. DON'T HAVE YOUR PHONE IN THE ROOM AT ALL WHILE YOU SLEEP – CHARGE IT IN ANOTHER ROOM AT NIGHT.

3. **HAVE A TECHNOLOGY-FREE ZONE IN YOUR HOUSE** E.G. THE KITCHEN OR DINING ROOM TABLE WHERE YOU EAT YOUR MEALS.

4. **UNPLUG YOUR WIFI AT CERTAIN TIMES** TO LIMIT ACCESS FOR ALL FAMILY MEMBERS.

5. **HAVE A TECHNOLOGY-FREE HOUR DURING YOUR DAY.**

6. **PRACTISE DELAYING YOUR SMARTPHONE INTERACTION** WHEN YOU THINK OF REACHING FOR IT, WAIT ANOTHER TEN MINUTES.

7. **INTRODUCE A 'TECHNOLOGY WEEK-END' REWARD SYSTEM FOR CHILDREN** GIVING THEM LIMITED ACCESS TO TECHNOLOGY FOR GOOD BEHAVIOUR, OR AT THE WEEKENDS ONLY.

8. **PRACTISE A SCREEN-FREE SUNDAY**

9. **PRACTISE NOT LOOKING UP** EVERYTHING YOU WANT TO KNOW AS IT OCCURS TO YOU ON YOUR SMARTPHONE.

10. **IF YOU ARE OUT FOR DINNER OR FOR A SOCIAL GATHERING** CHALLENGE YOURSELF NOT TO LOOK AT YOUR PHONE FOR THE WHOLE EVENING, BUT TO KEEP IT IN YOUR POCKET OR BAG.

LEARNING TO REST AND RECOVER

How often do you come home from work with your brain still processing the events of that day? Do you find it hard to unwind after a long day spent looking after children, when they are finally in bed? Do work or family thoughts and worries wake you during the night? How many of us can say they are well and truly rested by the time Monday morning rolls around?

Learning to switch off is a skill that we can learn with practice. In much the same way as a racing car takes a 'pit stop' to refuel and repair, we too need opportunities for rest and recovery during our day. The car with the best 'pit stop' strategy is more likely to win the race, so factoring in some moments to recharge is actually more productive. When training we had designated rest days when we didn't train at all and made a conscious effort to recover. I was happy doing this because I knew that it could improve my performance the next day.

After retiring I didn't find the resting (or doing nothing) so easy. It took time to learn that it was okay to do nothing sometimes, to not have my weekends scheduled to the hilt. The goal isn't trying to get around a track as fast as I can any more; now it's about being a better person and being more productive.

Resting is an equal part of the total process required to build strength, endurance and muscle and focus to perform.

Relaxation and downtime is not just about meditation, it's about **finding something that works for you** (see 'Scheduling in Yourself' p.61). Some of you may consider a brisk walk your way of recovering or relaxing while others may prefer a long bath and a good book, or a coffee and catch-up with a friend. Some of us need silence and others music. One cold morning I stopped at a petrol station and saw a homeless man. I bought him a cup of tea and felt better for the rest of the day. The takeaway from this is that doing a good deed or 'giving back' can be as good for recovery as taking ten minutes out. It increases self-esteem and stimulates the release of endorphins, which have been linked to improved body functions. Whatever the action, make the conscious decision to take that time for yourself, a walk in an open space, listening to music or a podcast or simply reading the daily paper.

RELAXATION TECHNIQUES

Using practical relaxation techniques such as visualisation, or focusing on breathing, can really work when you are experiencing broken sleep or anxiety. When I was in the 'call room' before a big race, I would imagine I was on a beach with waves coming in and out. The waves coming in (my in-breaths) were confidence and the waves going out (my out-breaths) were negative thoughts. Before I knew it I was focused on my breathing and relaxed. You could also visualise a feather on the end of your nose; the breaths you take must be slow and gentle so as not to dislodge the feather.

I also find this five-minute method very effective: place one hand on your chest and the other on your diaphragm and breathe in for three seconds and out for five.

REDUCE THE NOISE

By noise, I don't just mean the bombardment of our senses that we are exposed to on a daily basis through media and technology; our **internal dialogue** can be louder than anything else. I used to call my inner voice 'Radio Gillick' and I hated being stuck with him, especially in my car. It's easy to switch off the radio or TV but the internal voice is more difficult to quieten down. Unfortunately it's often telling you negative things like you'll never succeed at something, or making you write shopping lists in your head when stopped at traffic lights.

I practise five minutes of complete silence every day. If I'm in the car, I'll turn off the radio. If I'm at home, I'll meditate or just lie down and close my eyes in silence, which helps me to focus.

FIVE TIPS FOR MEDITATING

1

GET AWAY FROM ANY NOISE

Find a quiet space and put in ear plugs or ear phones with no music to block out external sounds.

2

FIND COMFORTABLE SURROUNDINGS

where you are relaxed and can rest your eyes.

3

TAKE STEPS TO ENSURE YOU WON'T BE INTERRUPTED BY ANY DISTRACTIONS

E.g. put your phone on airplane mode.

4

FOCUS ON YOUR BREATH,

and breathe to a nice slow rhythm. You may get distracted – that's okay, just refocus, reset and continue.

5

DO A BODY SCAN

Focus on different parts of your body, starting with your toes, and tense and let go. Work upwards to your head.

Tips for recovery:

1. **ENGAGE WITH PEOPLE**
   WHETHER FOR A LIGHT-HEARTED CHAT, OR TO SHARE YOUR PROBLEMS, WHICH WILL IMMEDIATELY DIMINISH THEM (AND HOPEFULLY QUIETEN THAT INNER VOICE FEEDING YOU NEGATIVE VIBES).

2. **EAT AROUND A TABLE**
   WITH YOUR FAMILY OR PARTNER AND CREATE DIALOGUE.

3. **PLAN YOUR HOLIDAYS**
   SO YOU HAVE SOMETHING TO LOOK FORWARD TO.

4. **PRACTISE A FEW MINUTES**
   OF SILENCE EACH DAY.

5. **MEDITATE**

MEDITATION

Mediation is often described as a way of training the mind in the same way that exercise trains the body. It can help you learn how to re-direct unhelpful thoughts and become calmer. There are lots of apps you can get to show you how to get started, but if you really want to avoid your phone they aren't necessary.

The benefits of daily mediation are huge, including:

1. **STRESS REDUCTION**
   MEDITATION GIVES US THE SPACE AND CLARITY TO DETERMINE WHAT ARE VALID DEMANDS AND INCREASE THE RESOURCES REQUIRED TO MANAGE THOSE DEMANDS.

2. **LOWER BLOOD PRESSURE**
   BY DECREASING STRESS AND INCREASING OUR COPING ABILITY, BLOOD PRESSURE DECREASES.

3. **POSITIVE OUTLOOK**
   RESEARCH SUGGESTS THAT 30 MINUTES OF MEDITATION IMPROVES ANXIETY AND DEPRESSIVE SYMPTOMS.

4. **SELF-AWARENESS**
   CONNECTING WITH OURSELVES CAN HELP US MANAGE OUR LIVES MORE EFFECTIVELY.

5. **INCREASED ATTENTION SPAN**
   HELPS US LEARN HOW TO DISCIPLINE OURSELVES AND ADDRESS TASKS WITH MORE FOCUS, IMPROVING EFFICIENCY.

6. **IMPROVES SLEEP**
   IT SLOWS DOWN THE MIND, AIDING BETTER SLEEP, AND IMPROVES OUR SLOW SLEEP WAVE PATTERN.

THE BANK OF SLEEP

In my training days, a good night's sleep was considered a weapon; a sure conduit to good performance the following day. Sleep gave me energy and ample time for my body to recover from a hard day's training. I developed a pre-bed routine which included a snack and a cup of tea 90 minutes before bed, a light stretch and a self-massage on a foam roller, reading a book and then lights out at roughly the same time each night. I also knew that if I slept well on consecutive nights, I might gain .1 or .2 on my sprint time.

Back then I recognised the importance of a pre-bed routine, and now that I'm a dad, that importance is highlighted even more. Our baby son Oscar sleeps much better when he has his routine of bath, bottle, music and a dark room. It's no different for us adults.

At the height of my depression, my sleep was severely broken and any semblance of routine was gone. My mind was pre-occupied with worry, I was restless, talking in my sleep and as a result, constantly tired and moody. The day after was then shot – I had no motivation and made poor food choices, craving high-sugar foods instead of my usual balanced diet to combat the exhaustion. Soon I found myself in a cycle of bad lifestyle decisions.

Sleep has been one of the last pieces of the puzzle to fall into place for me. In those difficult years, I underestimated its impact on my life and its importance for my body's recovery. I truly believe it's a commodity and should be viewed as something that adds value.

Think of it as a bank – the more you get, the more assets you have. We all know how it feels to be tired and how that can affect our mood, health, how we eat and our relationships. When we sleep well we make better choices and vice versa.

HOW MUCH SLEEP DO WE NEED?

We spend up to one-third of our lives sleeping but as the line between work and non-work becomes ever more blurred, the number of hours and the quality of our sleep each night is often inconsistent. Experts recommend between seven to nine hours of sleep a night with eight hours being optimal. But it's not just a question of hours; the condition of your sleep is also important.

* **Do you wake up feeling refreshed?**
* **Do you fall asleep within half an hour of getting into bed?**

If you've answered yes to those questions you're probably getting the sleep you need. If not, there's likely to be something in your lifestyle affecting your sleeping pattern: alcohol, eating late at night, drinking lots of fluids before bed, using electronic devices and anxiety all affect sleep patterns. If you get into bad habits such as watching TV until all hours then waking up late and skipping breakfast, then all kinds of rhythms are going to go out of whack. We'll get on to those rhythms in the next bit.

By making conscious changes to our lifestyles, we make direct changes to how we sleep and to our ability to achieve what we set out to do.

RESPECT YOUR RHYTHMS

You know you're supposed to get a good night's sleep but ... you've just got to finish something for work, you're making the kids' lunches at midnight because you've been binge-watching your new favourite Netflix show or you're enjoying a few beers with your friends. We've all been there. A late night here and there won't do much damage but consistent interruptions to your sleep will. Our circadian rhythm is our 24-hour internal clock or natural sleep–wake cycle and plays a part in everything

from hormone levels to body temperature. When the cycle is disrupted, everything is thrown out of sync. Have you ever enjoyed a lie-in only to find you feel more tired or drowsy during the day? Maintaining a consistent sleep schedule, going to bed and waking at roughly the same time every day, is fundamental to optimal health.

GETTING A GOOD NIGHT'S SLEEP

Getting a good night's sleep sounds like something glib the doctor orders for you if you are run down or stressed. But as we've seen, it's not always that easy – I can bear testament to that. The good news is there are drug-free, positive, practical steps you can take that will bring you at least part of the way to that magical eight hours of uninterrupted sleep.

1. **DEVELOP A PRE-BED ROUTINE**
   IT COULD INVOLVE A BATH, A HOT DRINK AND SMALL SNACK LIKE A CRACKER (BUT SEE POINT 5), READING A BOOK, A CASUAL STRETCH ...

2. **CREATE A QUIET AND DARK ENVIRONMENT IN YOUR BEDROOM**
   IT SHOULD BE PROPERLY DARK, LIKE A CAVE, SO IF YOU LIVE IN AN URBAN AREA

FOODS TO ENCOURAGE OR
AVOID FOR A GOOD NIGHT'S SLEEP

AVOID:

CHOCOLATE

CAFFEINE

ALCOHOL

FIZZY
DRINKS

TRY:

HERBAL TEA

NUTS
& SEEDS

OAT
CAKE

GREEK
YOGHURT,
COTTAGE
CHEESE

MILK

WITH STREETLIGHTS OR DON'T HAVE GOOD ENOUGH CURTAINS, CONSIDER GETTING SOME BLACKOUT BLINDS.

3. **MAINTAIN A CONSISTENT ROOM TEMPERATURE** SOME PEOPLE PREFER A COOL ENVIRONMENT TO SLEEP IN, WITH THE WINDOW OPEN; OTHERS PREFER IT A BIT MORE COSY.

4. **MAINTAIN A NATURAL SLEEP WAVE CYCLE** WAKE AND SLEEP AT ROUGHLY THE SAME TIME EVERY DAY. THERE'S EVEN A 'BEDTIME' OPTION ON SOME SMARTPHONES WHERE YOU CAN SET YOUR OPTIMAL TIMES FOR SLEEP AND WAKING, AND THEN BE GENTLY REMINDED WHEN TO GO TO BED AND WHEN TO GET UP EVERY DAY.

5. **AVOID LIQUIDS AND FOOD** IN THE 60 MINUTES BEFORE YOU RETIRE FOR THE NIGHT.

6. **BE SMART ABOUT WHAT YOU EAT** BIG MEALS, SUGAR OR CAFFEINE IN THE EVENING CAN AFFECT YOUR SLEEP QUALITY.

7. **GET OUTSIDE DURING THE DAY** EXPOSURE TO DAYLIGHT HELPS THE BODY'S NATURAL SECRETION OF MELATONIN, WHICH HELPS KEEP THE BODY'S RHYTHMS IN HARMONY.

8. **DON'T USE PHONES** OR COMPUTERS OR WATCH TV WHILE IN BED.

9. **WIND DOWN** DAYTIME ACTIVITIES CAN BE OVER-STIMULATING. CLEAR YOUR HEAD, AND TAKE THINGS AT A SLOWER PACE IN THE EVENING IF YOU ARE IN FOR THE NIGHT.

10. **SWITCH YOUR PHONE** TO AIRPLANE MODE OR LEAVE IT IN ANOTHER ROOM.

11. **DON'T NAP** AFTER 3 P.M.

12. **AIM FOR AT LEAST SEVEN HOURS** OF SLEEP EACH NIGHT.

13. **IF YOU HAVE CHILDREN,** AND IT'S AN OPTION, TAKE TURNS WITH YOUR PARTNER IN ATTENDING TO WAKEFUL CHILDREN SO AT LEAST ONE OF YOU GETS A GOOD NIGHT'S REST.

BENEFITS OF A GOOD NIGHT'S SLEEP

There's really no end to the benefits of those precious eight hours a night – both physical and mental. I've listed a few of them below.

1. **REDUCES MENTAL FATIGUE AND STRESS**
   REGULAR DEEP SLEEP HELPS PREVENT ELEVATED LEVELS OF STRESS HORMONES CAUSED BY LACK OF SLEEP.

2. **BOOSTS MEMORY**
   OUR MINDS ARE BUSY WHILE WE SLEEP, STRENGTHENING CONNECTIONS BETWEEN BRAIN CELLS AND THE TRANSFORMATION OF INFORMATION, SOLIDIFYING OUR MEMORIES.

3. **IMPROVES COGNITIVE PERFORMANCE**
   GOOD SLEEP CAN CONTRIBUTE TO MAKING YOUR BRAIN MORE PRODUCTIVE.

4. **AIDS SPORTING PERFORMANCE**
   GOOD SLEEP CAN IMPROVE SPEED, ACCURACY AND REACTION TIME WHEN IT COMES TO SPORTS.

5. **MAINTAINS A HEALTHY WEIGHT**
   FEELING TIRED CAN INFLUENCE OUR FOOD CHOICES, MAKING US GRAB FOOD HIGHER IN SUGAR AND STIMULANTS IN ORDER TO GIVE US A BOOST.

6. **CAN HELP REDUCE INFLAMMATION**
   SLEEP BOOSTS RECOVERY AND REPAIR.

7. **BOOSTS THE IMMUNE SYSTEM**
   SLEEP, AS WELL AS A HEALTHY DIET, WILL MAINTAIN A ROBUST IMMUNE SYSTEM, HELPING US FIGHT OFF ILLNESS.

SWITCHING OFF AT NIGHT

Do you ever find yourself lying in bed tossing and turning, unable to switch off your thoughts, or waking up in the middle of the night and being unable to go back to sleep?

It can be incredibly frustrating watching the time slide by when you know you have to be up in a few hours and you are desperate to sleep. Try the 4-7-8 technique to get to sleep. This is a breathing technique developed by Dr Andrew Weil, a Harvard-trained doctor with a focus on holistic health. You can do it in any position but it's recommended to sit with your back straight while learning.

slide to power off

Cancel

4-7-8 TECHNIQUE

1

PLACE THE TIP OF YOUR TONGUE

against the ridge of tissue just behind your upper front teeth and keep it there through the entire exercise. You will be exhaling through your mouth around your tongue; try pursing your lips slightly if this seems awkward.

2

EXHALE COMPLETELY

through your mouth, making a whoosh sound

3

CLOSE YOUR MOUTH

and inhale quietly through your nose to a mental count of four.

4

HOLD YOUR BREATH

for a count of seven.

5

EXHALE COMPLETELY

through your mouth, making a whoosh sound to a count of eight.

6

THIS IS ONE BREATH

Now inhale again and repeat the cycle three more times for a total of four breaths.

Weil emphasises that the most important part of this process is holding your breath for eight seconds because this will allow oxygen to fill your lungs and then circulate throughout the body. It is this that produces a relaxing effect in the body.

Here are a few more ideas:

1. TRY CLEARING YOUR MIND WITH MEDITATION
SEE THE OPPOSITE PAGE, AND PAGE 69.

2. KEEP A NOTEBOOK BESIDE YOUR BED
JOT DOWN ALL THE THINGS THAT ARE SWIRLING AROUND YOUR BRAIN – BIG OR SMALL. TELL YOURSELF THAT YOU HAVE TRANSFERRED THE THOUGHTS FROM YOUR HEAD TO THE PAPER AND YOU WILL DEAL WITH THEM IN THE MORNING.

3. HIDE THE CLOCK
SO YOU CAN'T SEE THE TIME GOING BY.

4. IF YOU'VE BEEN AWAKE FOR MORE THAN 20 MINUTES
GET UP, MAKE YOUR BED (ADMITTEDLY THIS IS EASIER IF THERE'S NO ONE ELSE IN IT). GO DO SOMETHING LOW KEY SUCH AS FOLDING CLOTHES OR STEPPING INTO THE GARDEN FOR A FEW MINUTES. COMING BACK TO A BED THAT'S BEEN MADE SHIFTS YOUR THINKING SO THAT YOU CAN START AFRESH.

PODCASTS FOR POSITIVITY AND RELAXATION

* **THE MINDFUL PODCAST**
A variety of podcasts, all with the underlying theme of mindfulness, including guided meditations.
* **SLEEP WHISPERS**
Whispered ramblings and readings to help you to relax.
* **UNTANGLE**
People from all walks of life talk about incorporating mindfulness into their lives.
* **THE TED RADIO HOUR, NPR**
A narrative journey through fascinating ideas, based on popular talks given on the TED stage.
* **THE TIM FERRISS SHOW**
Bestselling author Tim Ferriss gets holistic life wisdom by talking to world-class performers from a variety of areas.
* **THE MINIMALISTS**
All about how to live meaningful lives with less; clearing clutter to make room for the most important aspects of life, like health and relationships.
* **HEADSTUFF**
Ireland's largest podcast network with fascinating podcasts on arts and culture.
* **MAD WORLD**
The Telegraph looks at mental health and why feeling weird is the most normal thing in the world.
* **HAPPY PLACE**
Fearne Cotton draws on her own experiences and shares advice from experts.

4. DIET

'I'm not dieting, I'm changing

my lifestyle'

We all have a relationship with food. We eat it every day, our lives and health depend upon it; our moods, and sometimes our relationships, are influenced by it. I often use the analogy of a racing car to describe the body – it won't perform well if it's being neglected or not getting the right fuel source. If you're not servicing your body well it's going to affect your output in terms of performance, energy levels, sleep, motivation and general vigour for life. Food is fuel for humans.

I enjoyed a very healthy relationship with food up until a few years ago. What I ate was directly linked to my performance on the track and gaining the edge over my competitors. I would jump out of bed in the mornings to get breakfast and was motivated to cook and consume healthy food. A few years ago, while I was strug-gling with depression and anxiety, my relationship with food became toxic. I had very little motivation to do anything, let alone cook, and started comfort eating. I wasn't getting enough protein or vegetables in my diet and thus craved carbohydrates and sugar that gave me short-term highs but terrible lows. Skipping breakfast and lunch became a regular occurrence and by the time I got home in the evening I was tearing the kitchen apart, eating anything I could find, ordering takeaways and overeating. I was caught in a vicious circle of negative eating that consequently affected my sleep, my moods and my self-esteem. I was convinced I was overweight and became socially isolated.

Thankfully, as I have made other changes in my life, food and I have 'made up' and I'm back cooking, appreciating and

enjoying it. It was a slow process that started with eating a good breakfast and eliminating the petrol station junk food I'd become fond of. I began getting up a bit earlier to prepare my porridge and my lunch for the day. After a few days of doing this, I started to feel better and was more motivated to continue eating well. Instead of shopping when I was hungry, I started to do a weekly shop based around a meal plan. The few good choices and changes I made soon became normal and the vicious circle became a healthy cycle.

Eating is not something we are born knowing how to do; it's something we learn. There's more to it than just putting food in our mouths – we need to understand the link between food and our brains and bodies, know how to strike balance in our diets, and develop strength in building routines and sticking with them. So much anxiety around food stems from confusion over what is the 'best diet'. Eating has taken a dramatic wrong turn in recent decades – at one end of the scale there is the huge proportion of obese people in the Western world; at the other are the 'aware' ones who obsess over carbs and fat grams. The wise mantra of 'eat less and move more' seems simple enough but can be difficult to follow in daily life, often because the way we eat is directly linked to our state of mind and to the way we perceive ourselves. Thankfully, there are ways to make adjustments to how we eat to foster

a healthy relationship with food that strikes a balance between the two extremes of overeating and over-restriction.

MINDFUL VERSUS MINDLESS EATING

When walking, walk. When eating, eat.

MINDFUL EATING
PAYING ATTENTION TO WHAT YOU EAT. SITTING AT A TABLE WITH NO DISTRACTIONS. CONSUMING A MEAL IN ENOUGH TIME. ALLOWING YOUR BODY TO TASTE THE FOOD. BEING PRESENT. EATING MEALS AT A TABLE WITH FAMILY OR PARTNER. KNOWING WHEN YOU ARE HUNGRY OR FULL.

MINDLESS EATING
EATING WITHOUT INTENTION. NOT PAYING ATTENTION TO THE FOOD OR HOW MUCH YOU'RE CONSUMING. RUSHING THROUGH YOUR MEAL. EATING WHILE DOING ANOTHER ACTIVITY.

HOW WE EAT

Everyone talks about the importance of *what* we eat, but what about *how* we eat? When I was growing up we ate dinner together as a family, around a table, every night. Sadly, this tradition is waning in many modern households. When you do sit down to break bread with other people around a table (not in front of the TV) it's amazing how much more meaningful the eating experience is. You eat more slowly (rather than just shovelling food in to sate your hunger) and are more aware of what you're eating.

So instead of seeing 'eating together' as a chore or another thing to fit into your busy schedule, consider it an opportunity to de-stress, a chance to find out how your kids are doing in school, or how your partner's day went.

How we eat is also related to our portion control. Have you ever eaten something, looked down only to find the plate empty or packet finished and wonder where it went? When we eat 'mindlessly' – in front of the television or while on the computer, for example – we are much less likely to realise how much we eat. This 'mindless' eating habit means you're more likely to overeat. Becoming more aware will determine your hunger levels, allowing you to eat only what you need and enjoy your food more.

WHY WE EAT

Of course we eat because we're hungry and to promote our energy levels, but the reasons we eat often have less to do with that and more to do with our emotions. How often do you stop and ask yourself if you're hungry? Are you reaching for the packet of biscuits because it might make you feel better? Are you bored, lonely, angry? Do you 'deserve' a treat because you've had a hard day?

In our culture, we have found ways to avoid difficult situations by consuming more food. We eat when we feel bad in the hope that it will 'cure' the feeling. We eat when we're lonely or when we feel shame, negativity or exhaustion. Even stress makes it hard for us to control what we eat – how often are you likely to choose a salad when you're under duress? Food is a crutch that can make us feel euphoric, but the more we overeat the worse we actually feel.

PRACTICAL TIPS FOR HEALTHY EATING

1
PLAN YOUR MEALS
in advance.

2
DO A BIG SHOP
every two weeks and stock up your
office and car with healthy options.

3
COOK IN BULK
and freeze.

4
LEARN SEVERAL HEALTHY
TEN-MINUTE MEALS
(see recipe section).

5
COOK A BATCH
OF GO-TO SAUCE
that you can add to a variety of dishes.

7
EAT AT A TABLE
without distraction.

8
SERVE OUT YOUR PORTIONS
try not to eat from the pot.

9
TRY TO EAT IN SILENCE
not with the TV or radio on.

10
CHEW YOUR FOOD.

11
CHOOSE A
SMALLER PLATE.

WHEN WE EAT

I'm not going to tell you when to eat during the day – we are all different with different routines and needs so there is no hard and fast timetable that each human being should follow. As humans our bodies are designed to go without food for periods of time – even the word 'breakfast' points to breaking the overnight 'fast'. Skipping meals, however, is a different story: it makes our bodies less able to absorb food, leading to overeating. Ideally breakfast should be satisfying enough to deter the need for a mid-morning snack and should be eaten within an hour of waking. Personally, I have found that eating every three hours is what I need to maintain a balanced healthy weight.

Studies have found that **eating within an eight to 12-hour window is widely considered to be the best eating routine,** and the one least likely to cause weight gain. The most obvious 12-hour window is morning until evening (8 a.m.–8 p.m. or thereabouts). Throughout the day we excrete waste products filtered by the liver and kidneys. This is why Time-Restricted Feeding (TRF) can be useful in maintaining a constant weight. TRF can be beneficial to people if they are grazers at night, as a higher daily calorie intake than energy output is the reason for weight gain. TRF reduces the likelihood of mindless eating, which in turn reduces the likelihood of energy in being greater than energy out.

Take a look at your 'eating clock' and consider mapping out a ten-hour eating plan that starts within an hour of waking and finishes at least two hours before bedtime.

Ideally, you should eat something before you exercise so your body has fuel to burn. In general, eating a meal high in carbs and protein and low in fat roughly two hours before you exercise is ideal. Think of a car. You need fuel to get that car moving, and your body is the same. Food supplies your body with the energy it needs to work out. Your post-workout meal can be equally important, and the more often and more intensely you train the more important this is. Poor recovery practices

FOODS TO EAT FOR A HAPPY GUT:

QUALITY PROTEIN
eggs, fish, meat, nuts and seeds

BANANAS

BEANS

BROCCOLI

ONION & GARLIC

Probiotic-Rich
YOGHURT OR KEFIR

BLUEBERRIES

FOODS TO AVOID:

HIGH-FAT FOOD

PROCESSED MEATS

REFINED GRAINS

SWEET OR SALTY SNACKS

ALCOHOL

can impact negatively on subsequent training sessions.

MOOD AND FOOD

The word 'hungry' seems to have taken on new meaning, no longer a physiological state but a mood. 'Hangry' and 'food swings' are the new buzzwords for those sullen side-effects from lack of food and, some believe, the wrong type of food. Serotonin is our happy hormone, converted from the amino acid tryptophan, which is found in high-protein foods. A lack of it is believed to contribute towards negativity, irritability and bad moods. We all know the feeling after we eat a sugary snack, that spike of energy followed by a crashing low; it's more of a sugar slump than a sugar high and can leave you feeling lethargic and irritable for hours. The same goes for caffeine and alcohol.

This rollercoaster is just one of the ways food can affect how we feel. By contrast, eating plenty of tryptophan-containing proteins (turkey, pumpkin seeds, warm milk), combined with some carbs (such as jasmine rice) in the hours before bed can help get that happy serotonin working, improving poor sleep quality, which has been linked with low mood and worse food choices.

GUT FEELING

Scientists are now referring to our gut as our 'second brain', and the latest research suggests that our gut bacteria may influence the serotonin we produce. The collection of bacteria living in our gut, dubbed the 'microbiome', is essential to many aspects of our health. The bacteria produce vitamins and break down our food; their absence, due to poor diets high in refined sugars, carbohydrates and processed foods, has been linked to a host of illnesses and conditions such as obesity and inflammatory diseases like psoriasis. In the book *The Psychobiotic Revolution: Mood, Food and the New Science of the Gut-Brain Connection*, scientists found that our gut instinct dictates everything, from our weight gain and immunity to our mood. By changing our diet to include fibre-rich vegetables and fermented foods, in other words 'gut-friendly foods', they discovered that we could help alleviate depression and anxiety.

WEIGHT LOSS

There's an information overload out there about weight loss. Some celebrities champion the virtues of carb-free diets; others swear by high-protein and alkaline diets that promote the reduction of acid-producing foods. One thing these fad diets have in common is eliminating a whole food group, a practice which is doomed to fail in the long run. By restricting food groups you are essentially cutting out nutrients the body needs. Carbs, for example, are 'brain food' providing the glucose our brains need to function. Under-eating for your body's needs can trigger initial weight loss, but you have to think long term. It has become one of the reasons many people struggle to make long-term changes and keep the weight off. It's all about consistency and calories – one meal is not going to make you fat, and one meal is not going to make you fit.

The hard fact is, losing weight boils down to one simple caveat: **you must burn more calories than you eat – there has to be a deficit.**

I'm not a fan of the word 'diet' as it sounds temporary; I prefer to think of our eating choices as a lifestyle decision, especially since there's no one-size-fits-all philosophy. But I do believe that the food we eat plays a vital role in our body mass, as does exercise. For example, someone who has been happily abusing their diet with no outward signs for 20 years shouldn't be surprised to find it catches up with them in middle age.

It might be better to ask yourself what you can do that you enjoy and can sustain.

* **Can you add in one better meal a week?**
* **Can you cut out the sugar midweek?**
* **Can you restrict any alcohol consumption to the weekends?**
* **Can you include a five-minute workout at home?**

The optimal diet for you is likely to change as the years go by, especially when you consider that, post the age of 40, metabolism slows down and we lose approximately 1 per cent of our muscle mass every year.

EMPTY CALORIES

Is there any such thing as an empty calorie? The answer is 'yes'. Have you ever got to the bottom of a packet of biscuits or a bag of crisps only to find you're unsatisfied and could keep going? There's a reason why they're called 'empty' calories – they rarely fill or fulfill. A calorie is a unit of food to be converted by the body into energy. Most food has other ingredients fundamental to our health such as vitamins, minerals, antioxidants, etc. When a food provides *just* calories and little else of value it's considered an empty calorie. There's a big difference in good and unhealthy calories. An avocado, for example, might have the same calories as a biscuit but your body does not use it in the same way. An avocado is nutrient-dense and contains 'good' fat, promoting your overall health. Convenience foods such as chips, crisps, biscuits or fizzy drinks are common sources of 'empty calories' and more often the culprits when it comes to weight gain, especially when the amount of calories taken in is bigger than the amount used.

DEHYDRATION

When you hear the word 'dehydration' you may picture a desert scene with a parched traveller crawling towards a mirage of a gushing waterfall. The surprising truth is that many of us with unlimited access to water are dehydrated on a daily basis. Shocking fact: by the time we experience the sensation of thirst, we are already dehydrated. Maintaining the balance of water in our body is essential for us to function properly. As well as regulating our body temperature, water carries essential nutrients, oxygen and hormones around our bodies and is the vehicle for the removal of waste and toxins.

Dehydration can cause dizziness, constipation and fatigue; it can also be mistaken for hunger, leading to a higher calorie intake. Even without consuming the extra calories, depriving your body of the right amount of water slows its ability to burn calories, leading to an accumulation of extra pounds.

The recommended daily intake of water is approximately 1.6 litres a day for women and two litres for men. A good indicator of whether you have consumed enough water is the colour of your urine: if you're well hydrated it should be pale. You can last for up to three weeks without food but only three to four days without water. So drink up!

NUTRIENTS: MACRO AND MICRO

Macronutrients is a term used to describe the makeup of the three food groups we all require for our bodies to function:

* **CARBOHYDRATES (for energy),**
* **FATS (to keep us sated) and**
* **PROTEIN (to build and repair muscle).**

Unlike **micronutrients** (vitamins and minerals), our bodies do not make or store macronutrients and so we require them in our diets. Macronutrients maintain the body's structural and functional integrity.

Your body needs only very small quantities of micronutrients for survival. Some are made in the body, and some are not. Those that are made may not hit the required amount our body needs, therefore food becomes the vital source. If your body doesn't get the small quantities of micronutrients that it needs, serious health problems can result. Getting the right amount of both micro and macronutrients is vital to overall health and wellbeing, and through a well-balanced diet this can be achieved.

Note: Alcohol is actually considered a fourth food group after carbs, fats and proteins, and it is possibly the one that tips the balance for people. Alcohol has 7 calories per gram, compared to 4 calories per gram of protein or carbs, and 9 calories per gram of fat.

MINDSET NUGGETS FOR HEALTHY EATING

* **BUILD a good habit around food.**
* **CONSISTENCY is greater than perfection.**
* **MODERATION is sustainable.**
* **INCLUDE PROTEIN in every meal.**
* **IT'S OKAY TO HOP OFF the wagon and hop back on.**
* **THINK LONG TERM, not quick fix.**
* **STAY ACTIVE.**

SUSTAINABLE FOOD

Today, one third of food produced globally is wasted. In a world where the UN estimates the world's population is to grow by a third to over 9 billion by 2050, this is a big statistic. We all have a role in creating a sustainable future and food has to be a part of that. How we produce our food is critical and in order to feed our children's children, we can all make little changes to help support a sustainable future.

I support Origin Green, an initiative led by Bord Bia, which is the world's first national programme to promote sustainable food production. From farmers to food producers, retailers to food service operators, the programme enables Ireland's food industry to set and achieve measurable sustainability targets that respect the environment and serve local communities more effectively.

Food companies who participate and achieve the set standards are awarded the Origin Green logo, so make sure you look out for them on your weekly shop.

DG STORE CUPBOARD

These are the essentials I try to keep in stock as they form the basis of so many good recipes. They are readily available either in the supermarket, or your local health food shop.

PANTRY

* Light olive oil
* Extra virgin olive oil
* Manuka honey
* Organic cider vinegar
  with the mother
* Organic maple syrup
* Bicarbonate of soda
* Wholegrain mustard
* Sriracha or other hot sauce
* Good-quality tinned tomatoes
* Brown rice
* Lentils
* Pearl barley
* Quinoa
* Tamari or soy sauce
* Tomato purée
* Tinned white beans
* Full-fat coconut milk
* 70% dark chocolate
* Chia seeds
* Ground chia seeds
* Coconut flour
* Super seed mix
  (mix together sunflower seeds, golden
  linseeds, pumpkin seeds, sesame seeds,
  pine nuts, etc.)
* Almond butter
* Tahini
* Dulse seaweed flakes
  or carrageen
* Noodles (preferably buckwheat)
* Pasta (preferably wholewheat)

FRUIT, DAIRY AND VEGETABLES

* Frozen berries
  (mixed or strawberries)
* Feta cheese
* Probiotic natural yoghurt
* Frozen peas
* Frozen soya beans
* White onion
* Fresh root ginger
* Garlic bulbs
* Medium Irish tomatoes
* Greens such as spinach
  or kale

SPICES

* Coriander seeds
* Cumin seeds
* Ground cumin
* Whole black
  peppercorns
* Ground turmeric
* Ground cinnamon
* Chilli flakes
* Allspice berries
* Ground smoked paprika

EQUIPMENT

* A good supply of Tupperware or glass
  storage jars for storing food prepared
  in advance for easy access.
* Resealable freezer bags (Ziploc or
  generic).
* Clean jam jars that have been washed
  in the dishwasher (i.e. sterilised).
* Mason or Kilner jars for storing pickles,
  etc. and for creating the DG salad and
  noodle jars. You'll find these easily in
  home stores, kitchen shops or Ikea.
* A slow cooker is a great piece of
  equipment that will really boost your
  prepping ability.

MEAL PREP

The recipes in this book have been thought out with busy people in mind. We don't always have time to cook from scratch every day so with this plan you can make batches of food when you have some free time that then form the basis of your meals during the week. This makes it easier for you to make good choices and avoid the temptation of the takeaway or quick-fix processed option.

The recipes that follow are building blocks for meals over the next fortnight but can also be prepared to order in a few minutes. You will encounter these key recipes over and over again as you progress through this section. Once you've made them a couple of times they'll become second nature.

I suggest you pick a day when you have some time, such as a Sunday, to do your weekly shop. Re-stock your car and office as well as your fridge so that it's easy to make good choices wherever you are. Then make the recipes in this section to keep you going during the week. While you have the time on your prep day you could also do the following, which come in super-handy:

* **Roast four whole bulbs of garlic and eight medium tomatoes drizzled with oil and sprinkled with salt at 150°C for 30 minutes. You can use the garlic in spice pastes, sauce, dips and broths. Tomatoes are useful for tarts, noodles, salads and sandwiches.**
* **Roast a chicken for easy salads.**
* **Chop up fruit such as pineapple/melon and place in a container in the fridge – you are much more likely to use it if it's accessible like this.**
* **Slice carrots and cucumbers and store in a container in the fridge for easy access.**

DG VINAIGRETTE

My classic vinaigrette – delicious over any kind of salad leaves. Make sure to label and date these vinaigrette jars.

Pour all ingredients into a glass jar, shake and store in fridge for up to 2 weeks.

INGREDIENTS

200ml extra virgin olive oil

50ml organic cider vinegar

1 tsp sea salt

1 tsp Manuka honey

INVERTED VINAIGRETTE

Making vinegar the main ingredient makes this dressing very sharp – perfect drizzled over cooked potatoes and vegetables.

Pour all ingredients into a glass jar, shake and store in fridge for up to two weeks.

INGREDIENTS

50ml extra virgin olive oil

200ml organic cider vinegar

1 tsp sea salt

1 tsp manuka honey

TOMATO SUGO

This versatile Italian tomato sauce is inspired by Marcella Hazan's classic.

Peel the onion and quarter through the root. Put the tomatoes, onion, butter and salt in a medium-sized, heavy saucepan over a medium heat. When the tomatoes start to bubble, reduce the heat to simmer. Cook for 45 minutes, stirring occasionally, until the tomatoes have thickened and the sauce looks shiny. Allow the sauce to cool slightly then purée with a stick blender. Portion up into six containers and pop in the freezer for later use.

INGREDIENTS

1 large onion

3 tins of Italian peeled plum tomatoes

100g butter

sea salt, to taste

RED SPICE PASTE

This paste is similar to the yellow paste (page 107) but with no turmeric; the addition of sundried tomatoes and paprika changes the flavour and colour.

(page 107)

Preheat the oven to 150°C.

Pop the whole bulb of garlic into the oven and cook for 45 minutes. Remove, and leave to cool. You can also use a pre-roasted bulb.

Put the cumin and coriander seeds, allspice and peppercorns into a dry frying pan over a medium heat. Cook for about three minutes, stirring often, until the seeds turn golden. Tip into the bowl of a mini blender.

Cut the roasted bulb of garlic in half through its equator and squeeze the cooked garlic into the blender.

Add the rest of the ingredients except the oil and blend to a smooth paste. Spoon the paste into a jar, top with oil, seal with a lid and store in the fridge for up to two weeks.

INGREDIENTS

1 whole bulb of garlic

6 tbsp cumin seeds

3 tbsp coriander seeds

2 tsp allspice berries

2 tsp black peppercorns

4 tbsp fresh thyme, leaves picked

1 tbsp paprika

2 tsp dried chilli flakes

2 tsp sea salt

150g sundried tomatoes

100ml organic cider vinegar

2 tbsp ground chia seeds

2 tbsp light olive oil

YELLOW SPICE PASTE

INGREDIENTS

1 whole bulb of garlic

4 tbsp cumin seeds

6 tbsp coriander seeds

2 tsp black peppercorns

2 tsp ground turmeric

2 tsp ground cinnamon

2 tsp dried chilli flakes

2 tsp sea salt

6cm fresh root ginger, peeled

100ml organic cider vinegar

2 tbsp ground chia seeds

2 tbsp light olive oil

This spicy, paste with a vibrant yellow colour pops up again and again in my recipes.

Preheat oven to 150°C.

Pop the whole bulb of garlic into the oven and cook for 45 minutes. Remove, and leave to cool. You can also use a pre-roasted bulb.

Put the cumin, coriander seeds and peppercorns into a dry frying pan over a medium heat. Cook for about three minutes, stirring often, until the seeds turn golden. Tip into the bowl of a mini blender.

Cut the roasted bulb of garlic in half through its equator then squeeze the cooked garlic into the blender too.

Add the rest of the ingredients, except the oil, and blend to a smooth paste. Spoon the paste into a jar, top with oil, seal with a lid and store in the fridge for up to 2 weeks.

BASIC BROTH

This great recipe is a must to have on hand. It's really versatile and tasty and forms the basis of several warming, steaming dishes such as ramens and soups. You can choose to make it beef or chicken flavour, or a mix of both.

You can get bones at the butcher's counter in the super-market or at your local butcher. Place the bones in your slow cooker. The bones should fill up about 3/4 of the slow cooker.

Chop your vegetables and garlic, no need to peel. You can also add raw organic vegetable scraps into your slow cooker. Fill the slow cooker with water up to the maximum capacity. Add the salt and vinegar and cook on low for 18 hours.

Strain the broth through a sieve into a large bowl and cool in the fridge. The broth will have a layer of fat on the top and gelatinise when thoroughly cool. Remove the fat with a spoon and discard, then portion the broth into six containers and pop in freezer for later use.

1.5kg Origin Green beef bones or free-range chicken bones or mix of both

2 organic carrots

2 organic celery stalks

1 medium onion

2 cloves of garlic

1 tsp sea salt

2 tbsp organic cider vinegar

water

SUPER GRAIN MIX

INGREDIENTS

pearl barley

brown rice

quinoa

green speckled lentils

Cooking your grains in advance works great for when you need to put a healthy meal together but don't have the time to cook them. These are prepared especially for freezing to use in recipes later in the book.

BARLEY

Place 2 parts of cold water to 1 part pearl barley in a saucepan, bring to the boil then turn down to a simmer for 30 minutes or until tender. Drain and spread out on a baking sheet to cool.

LENTILS

Place 2 parts of cold water to 1 part lentils in a saucepan, bring to the boil for 10 minutes then turn down to a simmer for 15 minutes or until tender. Drain and spread out on a baking sheet to cool.

BROWN RICE

Place 2½ parts of cold water to one part brown rice in a saucepan, cover, bring to the boil then turn down to a simmer for 45 minutes. Remove the pan from the heat and leave to sit for 15 minutes (covered), then spread out the rice on a baking sheet to cool.

QUINOA

Rinse the quinoa in a sieve under running water. Place 2 parts of cold water to 1 part rinsed quinoa in a saucepan, bring to the boil then turn down to a simmer for 15 minutes or until tender. Drain and spread out on a baking sheet to cool.

Freeze separately or mix together to make a super grain mix. For a single portion, measure out 125ml in a measuring jug or scoop up ½ cup, then freeze.

THREE-STEP COMPOTE

This tastes fabulous spread on wholemeal toast.

Prepare the berries by de-stalking and cutting any large strawberries in half.

Place all the berries in a saucepan, add the honey and cook over a medium heat for about five minutes until the berries are nice and soft. At this point mash the mixture with a potato masher until smooth. Then add in the chia seeds and continue to cook for 20 minutes, on a low heat, stirring occasionally.

Remove the compote from the heat and place it in a bowl, where it will continue to thicken for a few minutes as it cools. Store in an airtight container in the fridge for up to a week.

INGREDIENTS

500g mixed berries (blueberries, raspberries, loganberries, blackberries, strawberries ... or use defrosted frozen berries out of season)
3 tbsp manuka honey
2 tbsp chia seeds

BREAKFAST FAST AND SLOW

We all know how important breakfast is, but that doesn't stop us skipping it on busy mornings. Some of the recipes here are designed to be made on your prep day and others are more suited to making on a leisurely weekend. It's still possible to make good choices in a hurry; the trick is thinking ahead.

Great speedy options include:
* Porridge with fruit and cinnamon
* Gilly bread (p. 156) with mashed avocado (add chilli flakes if you like a kick)
* Greek yoghurt with seeds and berries
* Banana and oat smoothie (whizz together 1 banana, 3 tbsp oats and 150ml milk of your choice)
* Eggs on wholegrain toast
* Smoked salmon and other deli cuts

In this section, you'll find some other quick, easy ideas for getting that fix at breakfast time.

CARAMEL APPLE SLOW COOKER OATS

160g pinhead oatmeal (also
called steel-cut oats)

2 medium apples, peeled, cored
and roughly chopped

500ml cloudy apple juice

400ml milk of your choice

60ml maple syrup

2 tsp vanilla extract

1 tbsp ground cinnamon

½ tsp ground nutmeg

a pinch of sea salt

SERVES 4

It is important to use nutritionally dense pinhead oatmeal (also called steel-cut oats) in this slow-cooked dish. You can try the options I give at the end of the recipe to vary the flavours.

Put all the ingredients into a slow cooker and stir really well with a wooden spoon. Cook on low overnight (7–8 hours) or high for 4 hours.

When cooked, give it a good stir for a few minutes until the ingredients come together and thicken.

Serve with a swirl of maple caramel (p. 238) and some fresh grated or sliced apple.

Store leftovers in the fridge for up to one week.

DOUBLE CHOCOLATE
Leave out the apple juice and use 900ml milk, 50g chopped dates instead of apple and 2 tbsp of cocoa powder instead of cinnamon and nutmeg. Stir in choc-hazelnut butter to serve (see p. 153).

PECAN PIE
Leave out the apple juice and use 900ml milk, 50g chopped dates instead of apple and 1 tbsp ginger instead of cinnamon. Stir in toasted pecans to serve.

PEACHES AND CREAM
Use 900ml coconut milk and 3 fresh or tinned peaches instead of apples. Stir in almond butter to serve.

BASIC BREAKFAST BISCUITS

These simple biscuits are a great on-the-go breakfast snack. This is the basic recipe – you can add the dried fruit and nuts and spice of your choice. Use the chart on the opposite page for suggested flavour combinations. You may come up with some of your own!

Preheat the oven to 180°C and line a baking tray with baking parchment.

In a large bowl, mash the banana and maple syrup together until smooth. Add the rest of the ingredients. Mix well to ensure all of the dry ingredients are coated with the banana.

Let the mixture stand for at least 10 minutes to absorb the moisture from the banana.

Run your hands under the cold tap to wet them, then take approximately 2 heaped tablespoons of the mixture, mould into a cookie shape and pop onto the lined baking tray. Repeat with the rest of the mixture, wetting your hands as needed.

Bake for 15–20 minutes, or until the biscuits are golden. Remove from the oven, then transfer to a rack to cool completely.

The biscuits will keep for 3 days in an airtight tin but they freeze really well, so just take a couple out the night before to enjoy in the morning.

INGREDIENTS

2 bananas

1 tbsp maple syrup

100g rolled oats

30g nuts or seeds of your choice

30g shredded coconut

40g dried fruit of your choice

1 tbsp whole chia seeds

1 tsp spice or zest of your choice

a pinch of sea salt

MAKES ABOUT 20 BISCUITS

FLAVOURINGS CHART
FOR BREAKFAST BISCUITS AND BARS

	DRIED FRUIT	NUT/SEED	SPICE/ZEST
1	CRANBERRY	ALMOND – CHOPPED	ORANGE ZEST
2	DATE – CHOPPED	PUMPKIN SEED	GROUND NUTMEG
3	MANGO – CHOPPED	PISTACHIO	LIME ZEST
4	GOLDEN RAISIN	PEANUT	GROUND CINNAMON
5	CHERRY	PECAN	GROUND GINGER
6	GOJI BERRY	TOASTED SUNFLOWER SEED	GROUND CORIANDER

NO-BAKE FRUIT AND NUT BARS

These energy-packed bars are perfect post-workout or for a breakfast snack on the go.

Line a 20 x 20cm baking tray with baking parchment.

Soak the dates in hand-warm water for 15 minutes then put in a large saucepan with the almond butter, maple syrup, coconut oil and chosen spice or zest. Warm the mixture over a low heat until the coconut oil melts. Remove from the heat then blitz with a stick blender until the dates are thoroughly incorporated. Add the rest of the ingredients to the pan and stir well.

Press the mixture into your tray and pop in the fridge or freezer to set. Once set, remove and use a sharp knife to cut into equal-sized bars.

These will keep in the fridge for a week but also freeze really well.

INGREDIENTS

85g pitted dates

60g almond butter

3 tbsp maple syrup

2 tbsp coconut oil

1 tsp spice or zest (e.g. cinnamon or lemon zest)

100g rolled oats

25g puffed rice

25g nuts or seeds (e.g. chopped almonds or pumpkin seeds)

1 tbsp whole chia seeds

3 tbsp shredded coconut

50g dried fruit (e.g. apricots or raisins)

MAKES 15

SWEET POTATO PANCAKES

INGREDIENTS

INGREDIENTS

2 medium sweet potatoes

2 tbsp ground chia seeds

4 free-range eggs

1 tsp baking powder

½ tsp ground cinnamon or cumin
(depending if you want them
sweet or savoury)

1 tbsp coconut or light olive oil

a pinch of sea salt

MAKES ABOUT 12 PANCAKES

These pancakes are fabulous – flavour them with cinnamon and pile up with Greek yoghurt, fresh berries and maple syrup, or flavour with cumin and serve with turkey bacon, roasted tomatoes and crumbled feta.

Preheat the oven to 200°C. Once heated, pop the potatoes on a baking sheet and cook in the oven for 35 minutes. Allow the potatoes to cool, then peel off the skin.

Mash the potatoes well with a fork. Whisk together the sweet potato, chia seeds, baking powder and eggs until well combined, then add in your choice of spice and a pinch of salt. Heat the coconut oil in non-stick frying pan over a medium heat.

Drop large tablespoons of the batter onto the pan and cook for 3–4 minutes.

Flip each cake and cook for an additional 3–4 minutes, until lightly golden brown on the outside and cooked through.

SWEETLY SPICED MULTISEED BANANA AND HONEY LOAF

This breakfast treat is rich in honey so it makes a great post-morning workout treat. Try it toasted and spread with almond butter.

Preheat the oven to 170°C. Line a loaf tin with baking parchment.

Mash the bananas in a large bowl and add the egg, vanilla, olive oil and honey, mixing everything well. Stir in the dry ingredients and pour the batter into the prepared tin.

Bake for 50–60 minutes, until a toothpick or the tip of a knife comes out clean.

Allow to cool in the loaf pan on a rack before slicing.

INGREDIENTS

3 very ripe
medium bananas, peeled
1 large egg
1 tsp vanilla extract
80ml light olive oil
250g manuka honey
180g stoneground
wholewheat flour
60g omega seed mix
1 heaped tsp baking powder
½ tsp ground cinnamon
½ tsp ground nutmeg
½ tsp ground coriander

MAKES 12 SLICES

DG BREAKFAST WRAPS

INGREDIENTS

1 tsp light olive oil

100g baby spinach leaves

400g butterbeans

140g unsmoked ham, shredded

100g ricotta cheese

1 tsp ground cumin

140g Cheddar cheese

6 large tortillas

MAKES 6 WRAPS

You can make these protein-rich breakfast sandwiches in advance and store them in the freezer. Just stick in the microwave for a quick, filling start to the day.

Put the olive oil in a frying pan over a medium heat and wilt the spinach in it for 4 minutes. Remove to a colander to cool and drain.

In a large bowl, mash the beans with a fork or potato masher. Chop the drained spinach and add to the bowl along with the ham, ricotta and cumin.

Grate the Cheddar cheese. Divide the bean mix between the six tortillas, spreading it over half the tortilla. Sprinkle over the Cheddar and fold the tortilla over.

Cook the tortillas for 3–4 minutes per side in the frying pan until golden and crisp (you may need to use some more oil).

Cool completely on a wire rack, then cut in half and wrap in greaseproof paper. Either eat now, store in the fridge for three days or in the freezer for up to three months.

Reheat from frozen in the microwave on high power for 1 minute, rest for 1 minute then on high again for 30 seconds.

FILLING CHART

	FILLING SUGGESTIONS	CHEESE OPTIONS
1	COOKED SLICED MUSHROOM AND CHIVES	SHREDDED EMMENTAL
2	SLOW-ROASTED TOMATO AND PESTO	GRATED CHEDDAR
3	SHREDDED HAM AND SPINACH	GRATED CHEDDAR
4	COOKED SALMON AND RAW COURGETTE	RICOTTA
5	COOKED SWEET POTATO AND RAW SPRING ONIONS	CRUMBLED FETA
6	COOKED, FLAKED SALMON AND MIXED FRESH HERBS	RICOTTA

BREAKFAST QUINOA CUPS

INGREDIENTS

140g quinoa

1 tbsp light olive oil

280ml water

½ tsp sea salt

2 free-range eggs

2 egg whites (whites from a carton also work)

125g cheese (see chart for suggestions)

80g filling
(see chart for suggestions)

MAKES 12

This egg dish can carry your favourite breakfast combo, leftovers from the fridge or is delicious plain without cheese or filling. See the chart on the opposite page for my suggested fillings.

Preheat the oven to 180°C. Grease a mini muffin tin with olive oil.

Rinse the quinoa in a sieve under a cold tap for about 2 minutes.

Heat the olive oil in a saucepan over a medium–high heat and add the drained quinoa. Cook, stirring, for about 1 minute to let the water evaporate and toast the quinoa.

Stir in the water and salt. Turn the heat down to low, cover and cook for 15 minutes. Remove the pot from the heat and let stand for 5 more minutes, covered. Fluff the quinoa gently with a fork.

If using fillings, add your choice of cheese and filling to the quinoa and mix to combine. Spoon the mixture into the tin, filling each cup to the top. Bake for 15–20 minutes, or until the edges of the cups are golden brown. Let cool for at least 5 minutes before removing from the tin, then allow to cool completely. If not eating now, place the baked cups on a baking sheet, freeze until solid then transfer to a freezer bag. Microwave for 25 seconds on high per muffin.

BAKED EGGS

This is my simplified version of the classic *oeufs en cocotte* that uses up leftovers beautifully – see the chart on the opposite page for my favourite combos. These are easily prepared the night before and baked in the morning. Convert to an easy brunch dish by simply layering the ingredients in a large dish and baking for 15 to 20 minutes.

INGREDIENTS

1 tbsp soft butter

4 tbsp filling (see chart for suggestions)

2 free-range eggs

a pinch of sea salt

a pinch of cracked black pepper

2 tbsp crème fraîche

2 tbsp cheese (optional; see chart for suggestions)

SERVES 2

If you're making these to eat straight away, preheat the oven to 180°C.

Grease two ramekins or oven-proof teacups, glasses or jars with butter.

Add 2 tablespoons of filling to each ramekin then crack in an egg, sprinkle on salt and pepper, dollop a tablespoon of crème fraîche on each and sprinkle on cheese, if using. Place on a baking sheet.

The eggs can be baked straight away or prepared in advance, stored in the fridge overnight and baked first thing in the morning.

Serve with super seeded flatbreads (see p. 160).

FILLING CHART

	FILLING SUGGESTIONS	CHEESE OPTIONS
1	TOMATO SUGO (SEE P. 102)	GRATED CHEDDAR
2	GREEN PESTO AND BABY SPINACH	GRATED PARMESAN
3	RED SPICE PASTE (SEE P. 104) AND ROASTED RED PEPPERS	GRATED CHEDDAR
4	COOKED MUSHROOMS AND SPINACH	GRATED EMMENTAL
5	COOKED, FLAKED SALMON AND MASHED AVOCADO	GRATED PARMESAN
6	YELLOW SPICE PASTE (SEE P. 107) AND MASHED, COOKED SWEET POTATO	CRUMBLED FETA

MIXED GRAIN KEDGEREE

INGREDIENTS

4 free-range eggs

600g super grain mix (see p. 109)

500g smoked haddock

1 tbsp butter

1 tbsp light olive oil

2 tbsp yellow spice paste

1 small bunch of spring onions, sliced finely

2 ripe Irish tomatoes, chopped into cubes

a small handful of chives, chopped

a small bunch of fresh coriander, chopped

½ a lemon, cut into 4 wedges

SERVES 4

You could hard boil a couple of extra eggs to use in salad jars, snacks or sandwiches when preparing this nutrient-dense weekend brunch dish.

Place the eggs in a small pan and add enough cold water to cover them by about 1cm. Bring the water up to boiling point then turn to a simmer for 6 minutes. Remove the eggs from pan with a slotted spoon then run the cold tap over them for about a minute. Allow to cool, then peel.

Defrost your chosen mix of grains in a microwave bowl for 2 minutes on medium-low and allow to stand.

Put the fish, skin-side up, in a shallow pan over a low heat, and cover with boiling water. Allow to sit for 10 minutes, then take out of the water and, when cool enough to handle, pull the skin off and break fish into large flakes.

Put the butter, oil and yellow spice paste in a large frying pan over a medium heat. Add in the spring onions and tomatoes, cook for a couple of minutes, then tip in the grains and stir to coat. Add the fish flakes and heat through. Taste and season.

Cut the boiled eggs in half and put them on top, scatter with the chives and coriander, and serve with wedges of lemon to squeeze over.

SMOOTHIES AND SLUSHIES

Top with fruit and seeds and eat with a spoon as a smoothie bowl, drink as a slushie or pop in a water bottle and take on the go as a super-chilled juice. These dairy-free recipes are a versatile vitamin-infused start to the day. For each recipe, you'll need four 1.2 l reusable freezer bags. It couldn't be easier – just take a bag from the freezer, blend with your chosen liquid, and you're good to go.

SEAWEED, MINT AND LIME

INGREDIENTS

4 small pieces carrageen seaweed or 4 tbsp dulse seaweed flakes

800g fresh spinach, kale or Swiss chard leaves, rinsed and drained

juice from 2 limes

a bunch of fresh mint

½ a melon, cut into 3cm cubes

4 tsp matcha green tea powder

2 tsp spirulina

a mug of mint tea/350ml coconut water/water

MAKES 4

Soak the carrageen or dulse in warm water for 5–10 minutes.

Divide the seaweed, green leaves, lime juice, mint and melon between the bags. Add a teaspoon of green tea powder and ½ a teaspoon of spirulina to each bag.

Seal the bags and place in the freezer.

When ready to use brew a mug of mint tea and allow to cool, or use 350ml coconut water or cold water, and blend with the contents of one freezer bag.

SPICED BERRY AND NUT

Divide the ingredients between the freezer bags, putting the fruit and seeds in first, then drizzling on the honey and nut butter and adding a pinch of cinnamon.

Pop the bags in the freezer. When ready to use, brew a cup of rooibos tea and allow to cool or use 350ml almond milk, apple juice or just cold water and blend with the contents of one freezer bag.

INGREDIENTS

600g frozen berries

4 dried figs

**4 tbsp ground flaxseed
or super seed mix**

4 tsp manuka honey

**4 tbsp nut butter of
your choice**

½ tsp ground cinnamon

**a mug of rooibos tea/almond
milk/pressed apple juice/
water**

MAKES 4

SNACKS AND CONDIMENTS

We all enjoy a little nibble between meals, along with little dips and sauces that add flavours to our meals. Making a few healthier/lighter options can tide us over for a few days, and help keep us on track.

THAI LENTIL DIP

Serve with a sprinkle of spiced cashew and pumpkin seed trail mix (see p. 148) and a drizzle of extra virgin olive oil. Dig in with freshly toasted pittas or carrot sticks.

Drain the liquid from the lentils and place in the bowl of a food processor with three-quarters of the tomatoes including their oil, reserving the rest for serving. Add the almond butter, spice paste, lime zest and juice, then blitz. The dip can be kept in a sealed glass jar in the fridge for three days.

INGREDIENTS

2 400g tins green lentils

240g sundried tomatoes in oil

2 tbsp almond butter

3 tbsp yellow spice paste
(see p. 107)

zest and juice of 2 limes

MAKES 8 PORTIONS

ROASTED SHALLOT AND BUTTERBEAN DIP

INGREDIENTS

250g shallots

1 bulb garlic

2 400g tins of butterbeans

juice of 1 lemon

2 tbsp water

2 tbsp extra virgin olive oil

sea salt and freshly ground
black pepper to taste

MAKES 8 PORTIONS

Stir in a spoon of red spice paste (see p. 104) if you want a spicier dip. Delicious with crunchy raw vegetables or spread on crackers (try it on the seaweed and Parmesan seed bars, p. 145).

Preheat oven to 200°C. Place the whole, unpeeled shallots and garlic bulb on a baking sheet and roast for 25 minutes. Remove from the oven and leave to cool.

Drain the liquid from the butterbeans and place in the bowl of a food processor. Add the lemon juice, water and oil. Peel the skins from the cooled, roasted shallots, squeeze out the garlic and add both to the food processor.

Blitz the mixture to a fine paste. Add salt and pepper to taste and an extra tablespoon of water if a softer consistency is required. The dip can be kept in a sealed glass jar in the fridge for 3 days.

DG FERMENTED KETCHUP

Fermented foods are great for a healthy gut and this ketchup recipe is super-healthy compared to those sugar-laden supermarket versions. It also couldn't be simpler to make.

Just mix everything together and pop in a sterilised 1-pint Mason jar. This ketchup is actually really good just like this, but fermenting it for just a few days makes it even better. To ferment, just put the lid on and place in a dark and warm corner of your kitchen for three to four days, then store in the refrigerator.

This makes a lot of ketchup so I usually freeze half in a Ziploc bag for later use.

INGREDIENTS

450g organic tomato paste

60 ml kombucha

3 tbsp organic apple cider vinegar

2 tbsp manuka honey

1 tsp sea salt

2 cloves of garlic

1 tsp wholegrain mustard

1/2 tsp ground allspice

1 tsp soy sauce

MAKES 500G

DG FERMENTED PICKLE

This is a brilliant introduction to fermented foods that uses whey (the liquid that sits on top of functional probiotic yoghurt). Great in sandwiches.

Put the cucumber slices into a sterilised ½-pint Mason jar.

Combine remaining ingredients and pour the mixture over the cucumber, adding more water if necessary to cover. The top of the liquid should be at least 3 cm below the top of the jar.

To ferment, just put the lid on and place in a dark and warm corner of your kitchen for two days, then store in the refrigerator for up to 2 weeks.

INGREDIENTS

5 baby cucumbers, washed and sliced diagonally into 1cm slices

1 tbsp wholegrain mustard

2 tbsp fresh dill, snipped

1 tbsp sea salt

4 tablespoons whey (if not available, use another 1 tbsp salt)

250ml water

MAKES 5 PORTIONS

SEAWEED AND PARMESAN SEED BARS

INGREDIENTS

50g skinned whole almonds

160g jumbo oats, toasted

100g crispy rice cereal

70g Parmesan cheese, grated

50g pumpkin seeds

3 tsp seaweed flakes

4 tbsp chia seeds

½ tsp smoked paprika

½ tsp cumin seeds

½ tsp chilli flakes

½ tsp sea salt

½ tsp black pepper

3 large egg whites, beaten

150g almond butter

MAKES 16 CRACKERS

These bars are a healthy substitute for a savoury snack. Don't be put off by the long list of ingredients — you can whip them up in 30 minutes. Great to have on the go, or with a relaxing cup of tea.

Preheat your oven to 180°C. Line a 28cm x 18cm baking tin with baking parchment.

Roughly chop the almonds and place on the baking tray with the oats. Bake for 8 minutes and remove, but keep the lined tin for baking the bars, and leave the oven on. Tip the toasted nuts and oats into a large mixing bowl with the rest of the ingredients. Mix very well with a wooden spoon and press the mixture firmly and evenly into your lined tin.

Bake for 20 minutes then remove and allow to cool in the tin. Cut evenly into 16 bars. Store in an airtight container at room temperature for up to 2 weeks.

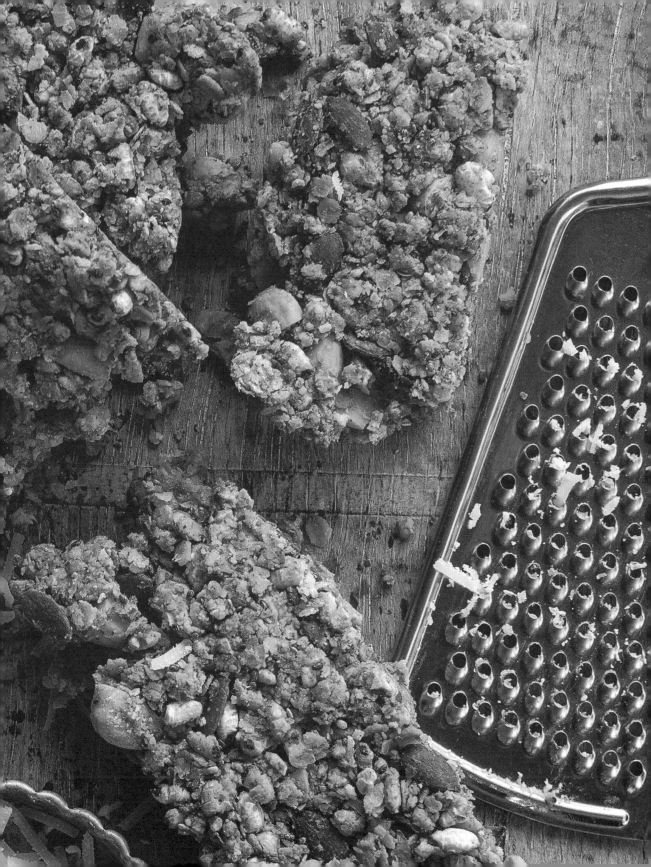

SPICED CASHEW AND PUMPKIN SEED TRAIL MIX

A savoury, spicy version of trail mix if you're not in the mood for a sweet snack.

Preheat the oven to 150°C. Line a baking sheet with baking parchment.

Tear the bread (if using) into bite-sized chunks, and pop in a large bowl with the cashews, olive oil and spice paste. Mix well. Spread onto the baking tray and bake for 10 minutes, then add the pine nuts, seed mix and pumpkin seed, mix again and bake for another 5 minutes.

Tip the warm mix from the oven into a fresh bowl and stir through the mango. Allow to cool, then store in an airtight container or resealable plastic bag for up to 2 weeks.

INGREDIENTS

100g super seeded flatbreads (optional; see p. 160)

150g cashew nuts

2 tbsp light olive oil

1 tbsp yellow spice paste (see p. 107)

150g pine nuts

300g omega seed mix (available from health food shops)

150g pumpkin seeds

50g dried mango, sliced thinly

MAKES 800G

ALMOND AND CHERRY TRAIL MIX

This is a delicious snack food full of nutrients. Take some of it in a Ziploc bag when you're heading out for a hike, sprinkle over porridge, or eat in handfuls from the jar.

Heat oven to 150°C. Line a baking sheet with baking parchment.

Mix the oats, oil, maple syrup, almond butter and vanilla extract in a large bowl. Pour out onto the baking sheet and pop in the oven for 10 minutes. Scatter the pecans and almonds evenly and bake for a further 10 minutes. Remove from the oven and allow to cool.

Put the cooled mixture into a fresh bowl and add the pumpkin seeds, sunflower seeds, cherries and goji berries. If using the chocolate, chop into 1 cm chunks before mixing in.

Store in an airtight container or resealable plastic bag for up to 2 weeks.

INGREDIENTS

200g rolled oats

2 tbsp vegetable oil

60 ml maple syrup

2 tbsp almond butter

1 tsp vanilla extract

35g pecans

70g almonds

35g pumpkin seeds

35g sunflower seeds

70g dried cherries

30g goji berries

100g 70% dark chocolate (optional)

MAKES 800G

GOLDEN GILLY MILK

**700ml coconut milk beverage
or almond milk
2 cinnamon sticks
a 5 cm piece of fresh turmeric,
unpeeled and thinly sliced, or
1 tsp dried turmeric
a 3 cm piece ginger, unpeeled,
thinly sliced
2 tbsp manuka honey
2 tbsp virgin coconut oil
½ tsp whole black peppercorns
350ml water
½ tsp ground cinnamon**

MAKES 4 MUGS

**A perfect, comforting hot drink to help with relaxation
and sleep.**

Place the milk, cinnamon, turmeric, ginger, honey, coconut
oil, peppercorns, and water in a saucepan and bring to
a low boil. Reduce the heat and simmer until the flavours
have melded, about 10 minutes. Strain through a fine-mesh
sieve into mugs and top with a sprinkling of cinnamon.

The prepared milk can be stored in a glass jar for 4 days
and reheated as needed.

CHOC-HAZELNUT BUTTER

INGREDIENTS

400g hazelnuts

100g 70% dark chocolate

1 tbsp maple syrup

½ tsp sea salt

1 tsp pure vanilla extract

MAKES 500G

If you've got a weakness for Nutella, here's my recipe for a guilt-free (well, slightly healthier) version.

Preheat oven to 175°C. Place the hazelnuts on a baking tray lined with parchment and roast for 12 minutes until golden and a bit oily. Remove from the oven and let cool slightly, then transfer to a clean, slightly damp tea towel and use your hands to roll the nuts around to remove most of the skins.

Pop the hazelnuts in a food processor or high-speed blender. Blend on low until a butter forms – about 8–10 minutes total – scraping down the sides as needed.

Break the chocolate and place in a large microwaveable bowl. Set the microwave at half power then melt the chocolate in 30-second bursts to start with, reducing to 10-second bursts, stirring between each burst until the chocolate is melted.

Once the hazelnut butter is creamy and smooth, add the melted chocolate, maple syrup, sea salt and vanilla extract. Blend again until well incorporated. Pop in a sterilised ½-pint Mason jar and store in the fridge for 2 weeks, if it lasts that long!

SOUPS AND BREAD

If you want to avoid the need to grab a shop-bought sandwich at lunchtime then being prepared is key. The lunch recipes I've given are all transportable so they're perfect to take to work. If you are based at home you can just take one from the fridge or freezer when you get lunchtime hunger pangs.

LENTIL SOUPS

Follow the basic recipe of this lentil soup and change the vegetables and greens according to season. You can substitute pesto, yellow spice paste, wholegrain mustard or roasted garlic for the red spice paste. The soup freezes well in small portions.

Put the courgettes, leeks, potatoes, celery, garlic and lentils in a slow cooker. Add the spice paste and broth, cover and cook on high for 5–6 hours or low for 7–8 hours.

Turn off the slow cooker. Take 500ml of soup and place in a blender with the olive oil. Pulse gently until emulsified. Add back blended soup to the pot and stir to combine. Stir in the kale and cider vinegar. Cover and leave to stand for 20 minutes.

Spoon into deep bowls, sprinkle on crumbled feta cheese and herbs to taste and serve with Gilly bread (see p. 156).

INGREDIENTS

2 large courgettes, sliced into 2cm pieces

2 medium leeks, thoroughly washed and sliced into 1cm pieces

450g waxy potatoes (Nadine, Charlotte or Maris Piper), cubed

4 young sticks celery, sliced into 1cm pieces

2 cloves of garlic, peeled and thinly sliced

300g speckled green lentils

2 tbsp red spice paste (see p. 104)

2l basic broth (see p. 108) or 2 vegan stock cubes dissolved in 2l boiling water

100ml olive oil

250g kale or watercress

1 tbsp organic cider vinegar

crumbled feta cheese and chopped fresh parsley, to serve

SERVES 4–6

GILLY BREAD

This easy to make, yeast-free wholegrain bread is easily adapted with different flavourings and is a nutritionally dense addition to lunch dishes. See the chart on the opposite page for my variations.

Preheat your oven to 220°C.

Put all the dry ingredients in a large bowl with your chosen flavourings and mix together by dry whisking with a metal whisk. Make a well in the centre of the bowl. In a glass jug whisk together the eggs with the yoghurt and milk and slowly pour into the well of dried ingredients. Using your clean hand in a claw shape, mix together the flour and liquid until everything is completely combined and comes together into a ball.

Wash your hands then dust the counter and your hands with white flour. Turn the dough out onto the floured surface (the dough can be a little wet so dust with extra flour if needed). Shape into a rough rectangle about 4 cm high. Transfer onto a floured baking tray and brush the bread with the milk or yoghurt or olive oil using a pastry brush.

Bake in the preheated oven for 25–30 minutes, then turn the bread over for a further 5 minutes. To test whether the loaf is cooked, tap the back with your knuckles; it should sound hollow.

Leave to cool on a cooling rack. Cut into 10cm squares (for sandwiches) or slices. Leftovers can be frozen.

INGREDIENTS

500g wholemeal flour
(or a mixture of 250g spelt flour
and 250g wholemeal flour)
350g self-raising unbleached
white flour
100g seeds, fruit or veg
(see chart)
2 tbsp herbs or 1 tbsp spice
(see chart)
1 tsp bicarbonate of soda
a pinch of sea salt
optional extra
(see chart for quantities)
2 medium free-range eggs
350ml functional probiotic
yoghurt
350ml milk
milk/yoghurt/olive oil for glazing

MAKES 1 LARGE LOAF

FLAVOURINGS CHART

	SEEDS, FRUIT AND VEGETABLES	HERBS AND SPICES	OPTIONAL EXTRAS
1	SUPER SEED MIX		
2	CLOVES SQUEEZED FROM 1 BULB OF ROASTED GARLIC	FRESH PARSLEY	4 TBSP GRATED PARMESAN CHEESE AND BLACK OLIVES
3	SUNDRIED TOMATOES (NOT IN OIL)	FRESH ROSEMARY	2 TSP CUMIN SEEDS
4	CHOPPED ROCKET	FRESH THYME	1 TSP CHILLI FLAKES
5	GOLDEN RAISINS	GROUND CINNAMON	4 TBSP BROWN SUGAR

SUPER SEEDED FLATBREADS

Delicious, super-adaptable bread that's great fun to make with the kids.

Put the butter and milk in a large microwaveable bowl and cook on high for 2 minutes. Sift in the flour and salt and stir in the super seed mix. Using your clean hand in a claw shape, mix together the flour and liquid until everything is completely combined and comes together into a ball.

Put the butter and milk in a large microwaveable bowl and cook on high for 2 minutes. Sift in the flour and salt and stir in the super seed mix. Using your clean hand in a claw shape, mix together the flour and liquid until everything is completely combined and comes together into a ball.

Tip out onto a counter dusted with flour then knead for a few minutes until smooth. If the dough seems too wet, dust with some extra flour. Clean out the large bowl, brush with oil, put in the dough, cover with a damp tea towel and rest at room temperature for 30 minutes.

Clean the counter and dust with flour again. Turn out the rested dough and cut into 8 pieces, roll into balls, then roll each one out with a rolling pin into 3mm-thick rounds.

Brush a non-stick pan with olive oil and place on medium–high heat. Place one flatbread in the pan, cook for 1–1½ minutes – it should bubble up – then turn and cook the other side, pressing down if it puffs up. Keep turning until lightly golden on each side.

Brush each bread with olive oil and keep wrapped with a damp tea towel to cool. Then eat, fill to make a sandwich or freeze in a reusable freezer bag for later use.

INGREDIENTS

100g butter

370ml milk

600g plain flour

a pinch of sea salt

100g super seed mix (see p. 96)

extra flour and olive oil

MAKES 8 LARGE FLATBREADS

LUNCH SALAD
AND NOODLE JARS

Salad and noodle jars are the perfect work lunch – make a few at once and keep them in the fridge. You can easily double the quantities to make several jars.

EACH RECIPE MAKES 1 JAR.

HOW TO PACK A DG SALAD JAR

* A couple of tablespoons of salad dressing
* Chopped crunchy and cooked veg (lower water content like cooked courgette, potato and mushrooms or raw carrot, cauliflower and broccoli)
* Grains and legumes like brown rice, chickpeas, lentils, barley, quinoa and cannellini beans
* Proteins like cooked salmon, tuna, shredded chicken, tofu, crumbled cheese and toasted nuts and seeds
* Delicate ingredients (higher water content vegetables like radishes, tomatoes, red or green peppers and cucumber)
* A couple of handfuls of seasonal greens
* Torn fresh herbs

HOW TO PACK A DG NOODLE JAR

* Miso, stock or bouillon powder
* Extra flavourings like soy sauce, coconut milk, citrus juice, pesto or spice paste
* 2cm cubes of cooked veg or chosen proteins
* Rinsed, cooked noodles
* Grated thinly sliced raw vegetables like carrot
* A handful of fresh herbs
* Leave space for adding hot water and shaking

JERKED SALMON
SALAD JAR

INGREDIENTS

**3 tbsp DG inverted vinaigrette
(see p. 100)**
1 tbsp red spice paste (see p. 104)
**½ a scotch bonnet chilli,
thinly sliced**
juice of 1 lime
**100g cooked potato or sweet
potato, cut into chunks**
150g cooked brown rice
50g red kidney beans
100g cooked salmon
2 spring onions, chopped
30g green beans, thinly sliced
100g shredded kale/watercress
1 tbsp fresh thyme leaves
a handful of fresh mint leaves

Mix the salad dressing with the red spice paste, chilli and lime juice and pour into a resealable jar.

Add the potato or sweet potato.

Mix the brown rice with the kidney beans and add in.

Layer on the cooked salmon, the spring onion and thinly sliced raw green beans

Add in the shredded kale or watercress, then top with the fresh herbs.

Screw the lid onto the jar and store in the fridge for up to 5 days. To serve, turn the salad out into a large bowl or plate.

CITRUS CHICKEN SALAD JAR

Mix the salad dressing with the spice paste and the lemon and clementine juices and pour into a jar.

Add the carrot and celery.

Add the lentils.

Add the almonds and layer on the shredded chicken, spring onions and raisins.

Add the spinach leaves and top with a handful of coriander.

Screw the lid onto the salad jar and store in the fridge for up to 5 days. To serve, turn the salad out into a large bowl or plate.

INGREDIENTS

3 tbsp DG vinaigrette (see p. 100)

1 tbsp yellow spice paste (see p. 107)

juice of ½ a lemon

juice of 1 clementine

1 carrot, chopped into 2cm cubes

1 stalk of celery, sliced into 2cm pieces

120g cooked green lentils

50g whole almonds, toasted and roughly chopped

80g shredded chicken

2 spring onions, chopped

1 tbsp golden raisins

100g spinach leaves

fresh coriander leaves

TRIPLE TOMATO CHICKPEA SALAD JAR

INGREDIENTS

3 tbsp DG vinaigrette (see p. 100)

2 tbsp tomato sugo (see p. 102)

1 tsp red spice paste (see p. 104)

75g slow-roasted Irish tomatoes, chopped

75g cooked courgettes, sliced

160g cooked chickpeas (could be from a tin)

60g crumbled feta cheese or torn fresh mozzarella

100g red and yellow cherry tomatoes, halved

2 spring onions, chopped

100g rocket

fresh basil leaves

Mix the salad dressing with the tomato sugo and red spice paste and pour into a jar.

Add the slow-roasted tomatoes and courgettes.

Add the cooked chickpeas.

Layer on the cheese, then add in the cherry tomatoes and spring onions.

Top with rocket, then roughly tear the basil and put this on top.

Screw the lid onto the jar and store in the fridge for up to 5 days. To serve, turn out into a large bowl or plate.

PHO NOODLE JAR

INGREDIENTS

75g dried flat rice noodles

1 tsp sesame oil

14g (half a pot) Knorr Rich Beef Stock Pot

½ tbsp yellow spice paste (see p. 107)

½ tsp ground cinnamon or 1 tsp five spice powder

1 whole star anise

1 tbsp soy sauce or tahini

1 tsp fish sauce

Juice of ½ a lime

1 chilli pepper (Thai bird's eye or jalapeño), chopped

75g roasted or steamed carrots, chopped

80g cooked and thinly sliced sirloin or fillet steak, or pulled beef

2 spring onions, finely sliced

a handful of leftover raw carrot, thinly sliced

60g beansprouts

a handful of baby spinach

a handful of mixed fresh herbs (can include coriander, basil, Thai basil, mint)

Put the rice noodles in a large bowl, cover with boiling water and leave for 10 minutes. Blanch in cold water and drain, then dress them with the sesame oil.

In a cup, mix the stock pot with the spice paste and cinnamon/five spice then spoon into the jar.

Add the star anise, soy sauce, fish sauce, lime juice, chilli and then the roasted carrots.

Put the well-drained noodles into the jar.

Layer on the beef with the spring onions, carrot and beansprouts.

Add in the spinach, and top with a handful of torn herb leaves.

Keep the jar in the fridge until you are ready to enjoy at home or at work. This will be perfect stored for 4 days.

Remove the noodle jar from the fridge 10 minutes before eating. Boil a kettle. Pour in boiled water to halfway up the level of the ingredients then stir well with a fork, cover and let sit for 5 minutes.

Give a quick shake, turn out into a bowl or eat from the jar.

GINGER SOBA CHICKEN NOODLE JAR

Bring a pot of unsalted water to the boil. Add the noodles, reduce to simmer, cook for 6–7 minutes then blanch in cold water and drain. Dress the noodles with the sesame oil.

In a cup, mix the stock pot with the spice paste, ground spices and fresh ginger then spoon into your jar.

Add the vinaigrette or vinegar, soy sauce, fish sauce, then the slow-cooked mushrooms.

Put the well-drained noodles into the jar.

Layer on the chicken with the chopped spring onions.

Add in the pak choi or spinach then top with a handful of torn coriander leaves.

Keep the jar in the fridge (for up to 4 days) until you are ready to enjoy at home or at work.

Remove the noodle jar from the fridge 10 minutes before you want to eat. Boil a kettle. Pour in boiled water to halfway up the level of the ingredients then stir well with a fork, cover and let sit for 5 minutes.

Give a quick shake, turn out into a bowl or eat from the jar.

INGREDIENTS

75g soba (buckwheat) noodles

1 tsp sesame oil

14g (half a pot) Knorr Chicken Stock Pot

½ tbsp yellow spice paste (see p. 107)

½ tsp ground ginger

1 tsp ground turmeric

2 cm fresh ginger, peeled and grated

1 tsp inverted vinaigrette (p. 100) or organic cider vinegar

1 tbsp soy sauce

1 tsp fish sauce

30g slow-cooked mushrooms

80g shredded cooked chicken

2 spring onions, chopped

60g pak choi (chopped) or baby spinach leaves

a handful of fresh coriander

SPAGHETTINI NOODLE JAR

INGREDIENTS

80g spaghettini

2 tbsp extra virgin olive oil

14g (half a pot) Knorr Chicken Stock Pot

1 tbsp summer no-cook sauce (see p. 185)

1 tbsp tomato purée

a pinch of chilli flakes or cayenne pepper

60g roasted tomatoes

6–8 black olives, stoned and halved

a pinch of sea salt and freshly ground black pepper

40g grated Parmesan

30g crumbled feta

¼ red onion, thinly sliced

1 small courgette, grated

60g rocket

a small handful of fresh basil leaves

Bring a pot of salted water to the boil, add the spaghettini, cook for 5 minutes then blanch in cold water and drain. Dress the spaghettini with 1 tablespoon of the olive oil.

In a cup, mix the stock pot with the pesto, tomato purée, the remaining olive oil and chilli flakes/cayenne, then spoon into your jar.

Add the whole roasted tomatoes and halved olives, along with the salt and pepper.

Put the well-drained pasta into the jar.

Layer on the cheeses then add the red onion and courgette on top.

Add in the rocket leaves, then top with a handful of torn basil leaves.

Keep the jar in the fridge (for up to 4 days) until you are ready to enjoy at home or at work.

Remove the noodle jar from the fridge 10 minutes before you want to eat. Boil a kettle. Pour in boiled water to halfway up the level of the ingredients then stir well with a fork, cover and let sit for 5 minutes.

Turn out into a bowl or eat from the jar.

HEALTHIER TARTS

These tarts are a crisper, nutritionally dense version of quiche. They can be adapted to use leftover vegetables and are a great way to carry stronger flavours. Take a slice or two to work for lunch or for a picnic in the park.

SPINACH AND BACON FILO TART

Preheat the oven to 180°C. Brush a 20cm springform tin with oil.

Brush one side of each filo sheet with oil and layer, oil side down, in a circle from the centre of the tin and up over the sides, overlapping the sheets as you go.

Arrange the spinach evenly on the pastry and scatter over the cooked lardons.

Put ricotta, crème fraîche, eggs and yolk, roast garlic and parsley in a bowl. Beat with a wooden spoon until smooth then pour into the pastry case. Sprinkle on the Parmesan cheese.

Bake in the preheated oven for 35–45 minutes until just set (start checking after 35 minutes). Ease the tart out of the tin, leaving it on the base, and return it to the oven for 5 minutes to crisp up the pastry. Cool on a wire rack. Serve at room temperature.

INGREDIENTS

3 tbsp olive oil

8 filo sheets

200g wilted spinach, well drained and roughly chopped

120g cooked bacon lardons

500g tubs ricotta, drained

200 ml crème fraîche

2 large free-range eggs and 1 yolk

2 cloves of roasted garlic, chopped

2 tbsp fresh parsley, chopped

2 tbsp grated Parmesan cheese

SERVES 4–6

TOMATO AND CHEESE FILO TART

Preheat the oven to 180°C. Brush a 20cm springform tin with oil.

Brush one side of each filo sheet with oil and layer, oil side down, in a circle from the centre of the tin and up over the sides, overlapping the sheets as you go.

Arrange the slow-roasted tomatoes over the pastry.

Put the ricotta, crème fraîche, eggs and yolk, spice paste and parsley into a bowl. Beat with a wooden spoon until smooth then pour into the pastry case. Sprinkle on the feta cheese.

Bake in the preheated oven for 35–45 minutes until just set (start checking after 35 minutes). Ease the tart out of the tin, leaving it on the base, and return it to the oven for 5 minutes to crisp up the pastry. Cool on a wire rack. Serve at room temperature.

INGREDIENTS

3 tbsp olive oil

8 filo sheets

200g slow-roasted tomatoes, roughly chopped

500g tubs ricotta, drained

200 ml crème fraîche

2 large free-range eggs and 1 yolk

1 tbsp red spice paste (see p. 104)

2 tbsp fresh parsley, chopped

120g crumbled feta cheese

SERVES 4-6

SANDWICH IDEAS

These quick sandwiches can be made the night before you want to eat them. They use a mix of leftovers and healthy shop-bought ingredients. Each makes 1 large sandwich.

PRAWN, AVOCADO AND BROCCOLI WRAP

INGREDIENTS

2 stems tender stem broccoli, uncooked and thinly sliced

1 tsp wholegrain mustard

2 tbsp probiotic yoghurt

cooked prawns

½ an avocado, sliced

1 super seeded flatbread

(see p. 160) or wholemeal wrap

a small handful (approx. 75g)

Mix the broccoli with mustard and yoghurt and season to taste. Layer with the prawns and avocado in the flatbread and roll up your wrap.

RAINBOW VEGGIE SANDWICH

1 small organic carrot, grated

1 tbsp red spice paste (see p. 104)

½ a small cucumber, grated

2 tbsp probiotic yoghurt

1 large square Gilly bread cut in half (see p. 156) or 2 slices wholemeal bread

⅛ head of red cabbage, thinly sliced

½ an avocado, peeled and sliced

a handful of sprouts

3 slices tomato

a few thin slices red onion

a handful of seasonal greens

Mix the carrot with the spice paste. Grate the cucumber and mix with yoghurt then season to taste. Spread one combination on each slice of bread, then layer up with the rest of the ingredients.

GRILLED VEGETABLES WITH HERBED RICOTTA SANDWICH

3 tbsp ricotta cheese

a handful of fresh herbs (parsley, basil … whatever you have to hand)

1 clove of roast garlic, crushed

1 tbsp extra virgin olive oil

sea salt and freshly ground black pepper

leftover vegetables – courgette, tomato, aubergine or Portobello mushroom

1 large square Gilly bread cut in half (see p. 156) or 2 slices wholemeal bread

Combine the ricotta cheese, torn fresh herbs, garlic clove, olive oil, salt and pepper and mix until smooth. Slice the vegetables lengthwise, brush with olive oil and season. Place under a hot grill for 3 minutes each side.

Spread the herb and garlic-spiked ricotta on each slice of the bread then layer on the grilled vegetables.

SALMON BANH MI SANDWICH

Grate the carrot and mix with lime, oil, tamari, garlic and ginger. Slice up a couple of pickles and layer in the split baguette. Mix the sriracha with mayo or yoghurt and dollop over, then add the salmon and coriander.

INGREDIENTS

1 small carrot, grated

a good squeeze of fresh lime juice

1 tbsp extra virgin olive oil

2 tbsp tamari or soy sauce

1 clove garlic, crushed

2cm root ginger, peeled and grated

DG fermented pickle (see p. 144)

¼ wholemeal baguette, split

sriracha or hot sauce

1 tbsp mayonnaise or yoghurt

80g slow cooker salmon (see p. 210)

2 tbsp fresh chopped coriander

ROASTED AND SPICED CAULIFLOWER WRAP

Preheat the oven to 180°C. Line a baking sheet with parchment.

Toss the cauliflower with the olive oil and spice paste. Bake on the baking sheet for 15 minutes.

Mix the tahini with the lime juice and sriracha. Place the spinach, roasted cauliflower and pickles on half the flatbread then drizzle on the tahini sauce and roll up.

INGREDIENTS

¼ cauliflower, broken into small florets

1 tbsp extra virgin olive oil

1 tbsp yellow spice paste (see p. 107)

2 tbsp tahini

a squeeze of fresh lime juice

1 tsp sriracha or hot sauce

a handful of baby spinach leaves

a couple of DG fermented pickles, sliced (see p. 144)

a super seeded flatbread (see p. 160) or a wholemeal wrap

SWEET POTATO, APPLE AND CHEESE SANDWICH

Spread the sauce on the bread and layer on the rest of ingredients, drizzle on the olive oil and season to taste.

INGREDIENTS

2 tbsp spring or winter almost no-cook sauce (see pp. 185, 189)
1 large square Gilly bread cut in half (see p. 156) or 2 slices wholemeal bread
½ a leftover cooked sweet potato, peeled and roughly chopped
a handful greens, like baby kale or watercress
¼ apple, thinly sliced
2 tbsp crumbled feta or blue cheese
1 tablespoon olive oil

SUMMER CHICKEN SALAD WRAP

Mix the chicken, yoghurt and mustard with the rocket. Spread the summer sauce on the flatbread or wrap, pile on the rest of the ingredients and roll up.

INGREDIENTS

80g shredded cooked chicken
3 tbsp plain yoghurt
1 tsp wholegrain mustard
a handful of rocket
3 tbsp summer almost no-cook sauce (see p. 185)
super seeded flatbread (see p. 160) or a wholemeal wrap
a handful of leftover roasted vegetables
30g black olives, stoned and chopped

WINTER PROSCIUTTO AND PEAR SANDWICH

INGREDIENTS

3 tbsp winter almost
no-cook sauce (see p. 189)
1 large square Gilly bread (see
p. 156) cut in half or 2 slices
wholemeal bread
a good squeeze of lemon juice
¼ pear, thinly sliced
2 slices prosciutto
a handful of baby kale

Spread the sauce on the bread, squeeze the lemon juice on the sliced pear then pile onto bread with the prosciutto and kale.

SPICY TUNA SALAD SANDWICH

INGREDIENTS

a small tin of good-quality tuna,
drained
¼ red onion, thinly sliced
30g black olives, stoned
and halved
3 tbsp probiotic yoghurt
2 tbsp red spice paste (see p. 104)
1 large square Gilly bread cut
in half (see p. 156) or 2 slices
wholemeal bread
2–3 slow-roasted tomatoes
a small handful of fresh basil
and rocket leaves

Mix the tuna, onion, olives, yoghurt and spice paste together then spread onto the bread and top with roast tomato and herbs.

SMASHED CHICKPEA AVOCADO WRAP

Put the chickpeas, garlic and oil in a small bowl and smash with the back of a fork. Add the avocado, mint and spring onion and mash together.

Spread onto the flatbread or wrap, layer on the spinach and roasted tomatoes then roll up.

INGREDIENTS

5 tbsp cooked chickpeas

1 clove of roasted garlic

2 tbsp extra virgin olive oil

½ a ripe avocado, peeled

a small handful of fresh mint, leaves picked

1 spring onion, chopped

super seeded flatbread (see p. 160) or a wholemeal wrap

a handful of baby spinach leaves

2–3 slow-roasted tomatoes

GILLY BURGERS

INGREDIENTS

**2 large cooked beetroots,
peeled and cut into cubes**

4 tbsp super seed mix (see p. 96)

½ a red onion, chopped

3 cloves of roasted garlic

160g cooked quinoa

1 free-range egg, beaten

4 tbsp cooked lentils

1 tsp organic apple cider vinegar

**1 tbsp red spice paste
(see p. 104)**

1 tsp sea salt

**MAKES 4 LARGE OR
8 SMALL BURGERS**

Who doesn't love a burger? These veggie burgers make a great weekend lunchtime treat for the whole family. Make smaller versions as 'sliders' – great for serving as snacks if you're having people over.

Preheat the oven to 170°C.

Place the beetroot, seeds, red onion and garlic in a food processor and pulse a couple of times until blended.

Transfer to a large bowl, add all the other ingredients and stir to combine. With slightly wet hands, shape into 4 burgers (or 8 if you're making sliders) and place them on an oiled baking sheet. Bake for 10 minutes then turn and bake for a further 10 minutes.

The burgers can now be frozen for later or served straight away in a wholemeal bun with smashed avocado, greens, DG ketchup (see p. 142), DG pickle (p. 144)) and some leftover roast sweet potato.

ALMOST NO-COOK DINNER SAUCES

These pesto-like blended sauces use seasonal ingredients and are great on pasta but also good in salad dressings, as a dip, brushed on chicken breasts to bake, tossed with cooked vegetables or stirred into soups and sauces.

TAHINI AND BITTER HERB (SPRING)

INGREDIENTS

100g fresh parsley leaves

30g fresh mint leaves

50g rocket leaves

4 tbsp tahini

juice of ½ a lemon

½ a roasted garlic bulb, cloves squeezed out

4–5 tbsp extra virgin olive oil

2 tbsp water

sea salt and freshly ground black pepper

MAKES 6 PORTIONS

Put all the ingredients in a food processor and process until everything is well blended. Add extra oil if needed to get a smooth consistency. Season to taste.

Keep the sauce in an airtight jar covered with oil for 2 weeks, or freeze in ice-cube trays and just stir through your dish while cooking.

ROASTED TOMATO AND OLIVE (SUMMER)

INGREDIENTS

250g roasted tomatoes

1 red chilli, deseeded and roughly chopped

25g pine nuts

40g black olives, pitted

2 garlic cloves, peeled and crushed

a handful of fresh basil leaves

8 tbsp extra virgin olive oil

30g Parmesan cheese, grated

sea salt and freshly ground black pepper

MAKES 8 PORTIONS

Whizz all the ingredients together in a food processor until well blended. Add extra oil if needed to get a smooth consistency. Season to taste.

Keep the sauce in an airtight jar covered with oil for 2 weeks, or freeze in ice-cube trays and stir through your chosen dish while cooking.

ZESTY SQUASH AND ALMOND (AUTUMN)

Preheat the oven to 180°C. Line a baking sheet with parchment.

Toss the squash with a little olive oil, salt, and pepper. Bake for about 20 minutes or until soft, and allow to cool.

Toast the almonds in a dry frying pan over a medium heat for about 4 minutes until they are slightly golden and crunchy. Place into your food processor while warm.

Add the rest of ingredients to the food processor and blend until smooth. Add extra oil if needed to get a smooth consistency. Season to taste.

Keep your sauce in an airtight jar covered with oil for 2 weeks. You can also freeze in ice-cube trays and stir through your chosen dish while cooking.

INGREDIENTS

½ a butternut squash, peeled and cubed

4–5 tablespoons olive oil

sea salt and freshly ground black pepper

100g whole almonds

2 handfuls of rocket

zest and juice of ½ a lemon

zest of 1 orange

2 garlic cloves, peeled and sliced

100g blue cheese (Cashel blue or gorgonzola)

MAKES 8 PORTIONS

KALE, WALNUT AND FETA (WINTER)

INGREDIENTS

**250g kale, woody stems removed
and leaves roughly chopped**

100g whole walnuts

2–3 tbsp extra virgin olive oil

1 bulb roasted garlic

**2 tbsp fresh thyme,
leaves picked**

1 tsp organic cider vinegar

200g feta cheese, crumbled

**sea salt and freshly ground
black pepper**

MAKES 12 PORTIONS

Put the prepared kale in the bowl of a food processor.

Toast the walnuts in a dry frying pan over a medium heat for about 4 minutes until they are slightly golden and crunchy. Add to the food processor with the kale.

Cut the roasted garlic bulb in half and squeeze into a bowl. Add this, together with the rest of the ingredients, to the kale and walnuts and pulse for a minute or two to achieve a rough texture. Add more oil if needed to achieve a smooth consistency.

You can keep the sauce in an airtight jar covered with oil for 2 weeks, or freeze in ice-cube trays and just stir through your dish while you are cooking.

SHEET PAN DINNERS

These dinners are a godsend – everything goes on a baking sheet or roasting tray and you don't need to prepare any sides. They are one-sheet tasty wonders that will feed the whole family with minimal washing up afterwards.

THYME AND LEMON SPATCHCOCK CHICKEN

Preheat the oven to 180°C.

Put the chicken, breast-side down, on a large chopping board. Using a large, heavy knife or sturdy kitchen scissors, cut down either side of the backbone of the chicken. Remove the bone, open out the chicken, turn it over and press to flatten with the heel of your hand.

With a sharp knife make slashes of the chicken and rub the spice paste in with your hands, pushing it into the slashes.

Using a potato peeler, cut strips from the lemon and throw into the bottom of a roasting tray with the thyme sprigs. Reserve the lemon for later. Add the sweet potatoes to the tray and drizzle with the oil. Pop the chicken on top, breast side up. Pour the basic broth into the bottom of the tin and roast everything for 45 minutes. Throw on the prepared greens, squeeze over the juice from your lemon and cook for another 10 minutes.

Remove from the oven and allow to sit for 10 minutes before carving and serving.

INGREDIENTS

1 1.3kg free-range chicken

1 tbsp yellow spice paste (see p. 107)

1 lemon

5–6 sprigs of fresh thyme

4 large sweet potatoes, each cut lengthwise into 6 wedges

2 tbsp extra virgin olive oil

300 ml basic broth (see p. 108)

300g prepared greens (cabbage, kale, spinach, etc.)

SERVES 4

SHEET PAN
PRAWN BAKE

Preheat the oven to 200°C. Lightly oil a baking sheet.

Pull off the husks and silky threads from the corn ears and cut the ears in half.

In a large pot of boiling salted water, cook the potatoes for 5 minutes, then add corn for a further 5 minutes. Drain well.

Put the grated garlic, spice paste, paprika, thyme in a large bowl and mix with the butter, olive oil and mustard. Add the cooked potatoes, corn and prawns and toss gently to combine.

Arrange the sausage slices in a single layer on the prepared baking sheet. Evenly spread the dressed prawns, potatoes and corn on top.

Place in the preheated oven and bake for 12–15 minutes, or until the prawns are opaque and the corn is tender.

Serve immediately with lemon wedges, garnished with parsley.

INGREDIENTS

3 ears sweetcorn with husk

400g small Jersey Royal or Charlotte potatoes, cut in half

2 cloves of garlic, peeled and grated

1 tsp red spice paste (see p. 104)

1 tsp paprika

a sprig of thyme, leaves picked

30g unsalted butter, softened

2 tbsp light olive oil

1 tsp wholegrain mustard

400g raw Dublin Bay prawns, peeled and deveined

300g chorizo, salami or smoked sausage, cut into 1cm slices

1 lemon, cut into wedges, to garnish

2 tablespoons chopped fresh parsley leaves, to garnish

SERVES 2

SHEET PAN TUNA NIÇOISE

INGREDIENTS

4–5 tbsp extra virgin olive oil

3 cloves of garlic, peeled
and crushed

1 tbsp wholegrain mustard

3 tbsp capers (optional)

juice of 1 lemon

2 handfuls of fresh basil

sea salt and freshly ground
black pepper

1 red onion, peeled and
cut into 8 pieces

90g green beans,
topped and tailed

150g cherry tomatoes

90g asparagus tips

2 fresh tuna fillets
(approx. 240g)

90g artichoke hearts, drained
(optional)

50g black olives

Preheat the oven to 160°C.

Whisk together the olive oil, crushed garlic, mustard, capers and half the lemon juice. Tear in 1½ handfuls of the basil leaves and season to taste.

Put the onion and beans onto a baking sheet and add the tomatoes and asparagus. Drizzle two-thirds of the dressing over the vegetables and roast in the oven for 10 minutes.

Then place the tuna, artichoke, and black olives on the cooked veggies and squeeze over the rest of the lemon. Return to the oven and bake for a further 11–12 minutes until the tuna is cooked through. Pour the remaining dressing over the vegetables and tuna and garnish with the remaining basil.

SHEET PAN STEAK FAJITAS

In a bowl, combine the spice paste, chilli, cumin and half the lime juice. Slice the steak against the grain into 2cm strips and marinate in the mixture for at least 20 minutes, but 2 hours if possible.

Preheat the oven to 190°C. Pop a baking sheet in the oven to warm.

Add the onion and peppers to the steak mix. Pour onto a heated baking sheet and bake for 12–14 minutes.

Serve on seeded flatbreads with crème fraîche and the remaining lime juice.

INGREDIENTS

1 tbsp red spice paste (see p. 104)

1 tsp chilli flakes

1 tsp ground cumin

juice of 1 lime

250g skirt steak

1 red onion, peeled and sliced

1 red pepper, deseeded and cut
into 1 cm strips

1 yellow pepper, deseeded and
cut into 1cm strips

a handful of fresh coriander

2 seeded flatbreads
(see p. 160) or wholemeal
tortillas and crème fraîche or
Greek yoghurt to serve

SERVES 2

DG GRAIN BOWLS

These quick, filling dinners make great use of seasonal ingredients. Just layer up the ingredients in a bowl and you're good to go. No need to pack them tightly as they are to be eaten straight away.

EACH BOWL SERVES 2

HOW TO PACK A DG GRAIN BOWL

* Fresh herbs, nuts or seeds
* Sauce or dressing
* Fresh, raw vegetables or sprouted seeds
* Cooked vegetables and proteins
* Whole cooked grains

FISH TACO BOWL

INGREDIENTS

150g red cabbage, shredded

30g DG pickles (see p. 144), cut
into matchsticks

½ small red onion, peeled
and sliced

1 tsp yellow spice paste
(see p. 107)

100ml probiotic yoghurt

juice of ½ lime

sea salt and freshly ground
black pepper

300g fresh pollock or hake fillets

3 tbsp coconut flour

1 tsp chilli flakes

1 tsp ground cumin

3 tbsp light olive oil

140g cooked mixed grains (see
p. 109)

1 avocado, peeled and sliced

extra lime wedges, to serve

You could also serve these ingredients in a wholemeal burger bun instead of with the mixed grains

Preheat the oven to 60°C.

Put the cabbage, pickles and red onion in a bowl with the spice paste, yoghurt and lime juice. Season to taste. Coat the fish fillets liberally on all sides with the mixture, reserving some for layering in the bowl.

Mix the coconut flour, chilli, cumin and ½ tsp sea salt in a shallow bowl. Cut the fish into 4cm-wide strips.

Place a cooling rack over a plate and place in the warm oven.

Put the oil in a non-stick pan and add 3 strips of coated fish. Once the first side is golden brown and crisp, use a spatula to flip to the other side and brown. This should take about 4 minutes per strip.

When done, place the fish on the cooling rack in the oven to keep warm while you finish the remaining fish.

Warm the grains in the microwave for 2 minutes or in a saucepan for 5 minutes on a medium heat.

Serve the crispy fish on top of a bed mixed grains with the remaining spiced cabbage and add some avocado slices with lime quarters on top.

TUNA POKE BOWL

First, get your rice on. Put in a saucepan with 450ml cold water, bring to the boil then simmer, covered, for 45 minutes.

When the rice is cooking, combine the soy sauce, sesame oil, vinegar, ginger, garlic, seaweed flakes and sesame seeds in a bowl, and stir well to combine. Add the tuna cubes and marinate for about 30 minutes in the refrigerator.

Cook the beans in salted boiling water for 4 minutes then drain.

Mix the siracha and the yoghurt.

Put the rice in your bowl, add the tuna then pile on the beans, pickled ginger or pineapple, radishes, spring onions, and avocado. Top with a sprinkle of coriander and a drizzle of spicy yoghurt.

INGREDIENTS

140g brown rice

3 tbsp soy sauce

1 tbsp sesame oil

1 tbsp organic cider vinegar

2 cm fresh ginger, peeled and grated

½ a garlic clove, peeled and grated

1 tsp seaweed flakes

1 tsp black sesame seeds

200g very fresh tuna, diced into ½-inch cubes

100g fresh green beans, topped and tailed

1 tbsp sriracha or hot sauce

2 tbsp probiotic yoghurt

20g Japanese pickled ginger or thinly sliced fresh pineapple

4 radishes, thinly sliced

2 spring onions, sliced on the diagonal

1 avocado, peeled and thinly sliced

a small handful of fresh coriander leaves

PORK STEAK FILLET BARLEY BOWL

INGREDIENTS

300g pork steak

1 tbsp red spice paste
(see p. 104)

120g green beans, topped and
tailed and sliced on the diagonal

extra virgin olive oil

2 cloves of roasted garlic,
crushed

1 tbsp seed mix

2 handfuls of fresh spinach

4 tbsp tomato sugo (see p. 102)

240g cooked barley

30g sprouted seeds

4 tbsp fresh parsley leaves

2 tbsp crumbled feta

Preheat the oven to 190°C.

Trim any sinew from the pork steak and rub with the red spice paste. Place the fillet on a baking sheet and cook for 30 minutes.

Sauté the green beans over a medium heat in olive oil for 4 minutes then add the garlic and seeds and cook for a further minute. Remove from the pan and keep warm. Wilt the spinach in the pan for a couple of minutes, remove from the pan and keep warm. Warm the tomato sugo in the same pan. When cooked, slice the pork into 2cm slices.

Heat the cooked barley in the microwave for 2 minutes. Put in your bowl then pile the spinach, beans, sprouted seeds and sliced pork on top with a sprinkle of herbs, feta and a drizzle of sugo.

SPICED CHICKPEA BUDDHA BOWL

Preheat the oven to 190C.

Toss the sweet potatoes, onion and broccoli in oil, place on a baking sheet and cook for 15 minutes.

Toss the kale in a little oil, add to the baking sheet and cook for a further 5 minutes. Mix the chickpeas with the spice paste and 1 tbsp oil and sauté in a frying pan over medium heat for 8 minutes, stirring frequently.

In a small bowl, mix the tahini with the maple syrup and lemon juice. Add hot water until a pourable sauce is formed.

Microwave the quinoa for 2 minutes. Put in a bowl then pile on (or beautifully display) the roasted veg and spiced chickpeas with a sprinkle of herbs and a drizzle of tahini sauce.

INGREDIENTS

2 large sweet potatoes, cut into cubes

½ a red onion, cut into wedges

225g tender stem broccoli, sliced on the diagonal

extra virgin olive oil

2 big handfuls kale, washed and larger stems removed

1 tin chickpeas, drained and rinsed

1 tbsp yellow spice paste (see p. 107)

50g tahini

1 tbsp maple syrup

juice of ½ a lemon

200g cooked quinoa

a small handful of fresh mint leaves

MINDFUL MEALS

These dishes take a little bit of preparation but then use a slow cooker to easily produce perfect family dinners. Slow cookers are great for families as you can put everything on in the morning and come home to a steaming, tasty ready-made meal.

EACH MEAL SERVES 4

LEMON AND ROSEMARY BEEF CASSEROLE

The lemon and rosemary add zest and depth to this warming casserole for a winter's evening.

Set the slow cooker to low and put in the onion, squash, carrots, whole mushrooms, whole potatoes and then add the beef on top.

Add tomato purée, lemon peel, bay leaf, rosemary and seaweed to the stock. Stir in the cornflour paste with the olive oil and roasted garlic.

Pour the stock over the beef, and cook for 7–10 hours. The stew can be frozen in portions at this stage, then defrosted and reheated. Remove the lemon peel and bay leaf then serve with cooked lentils, Gilly bread (see p. 156) and wilted greens.

INGREDIENTS

1 red onion, peeled and thinly sliced

1 butternut squash, peeled and cubed

4 carrots, peeled and sliced

150g button mushrooms

500g small Jersey Royal or Charlotte potatoes

800 g stewing steak, cut into 5cm cubes

2 tbsp tomato purée

4 strips of lemon peel

1 bay leaf

a few sprigs of fresh rosemary

1 tbsp dulse (seaweed) flakes or 1 piece of carrageen, chopped

300 ml boiling water mixed with 1 Knorr Rich Beef Stock Pot

1 tsp cornflour mixed with 3 tbsp cold water

1 tbsp extra virgin olive oil

½ a bulb of roasted garlic, cloves squeezed out

CHICKEN AND DUBLIN BAY PRAWN GUMBO

INGREDIENTS

1 green pepper, seeded and diced

1 small white onion, peeled and sliced

2 celery stalks, thinly sliced

100g okra (optional)

600g boneless, skinless chicken thighs

200g chorizo, salami or spiced sausage, sliced into 1cm pieces

1 bulb roasted garlic

1 400g tin good-quality chopped tomatoes

4 tbsp tomato purée

1 tbsp organic cider vinegar

2 tbsp red spice paste (see p. 104)

1 tbsp fresh thyme leaves

1 tbsp dried oregano

1 tsp cracked black pepper

1 tsp sriracha or hot sauce

200g Dublin Bay prawns

sea salt and freshly ground black pepper, to taste

fresh coriander, to serve

Anything with chorizo and prawns is bound to be popular with most people, especially kids!

Put the pepper, onion, celery, okra, chicken thighs and sliced sausage into your slow cooker. Squeeze in the roasted garlic.

Mix the tinned tomatoes and tomato purée with the vinegar, spice paste, herbs, pepper and hot sauce.

Pour the tomato mixture over the chicken, vegetables and sausage. Cook on high for 3–4 hours or low for 6–7 hours. In the last 15–20 minutes of cooking time, add in the prawns.

Stir well and season to taste before serving in a bowl with brown rice and fresh coriander.

SLOW-COOKED SALMON WITH SPICED YOGHURT SAUCE

This really tasty and super-healthy recipe makes use of any leftover raw veg you might have.

Cut a large square of baking parchment and press it into your slow cooker. This makes it easier to lift the salmon out later.

Place your choice of veg along with the star anise, coriander seeds and peppercorns on the parchment in the slow cooker.

Place the salmon skin-side down in the slow cooker.

Pour over the water then add the vinegar and salt. Cover and cook on low for 2 hours.

Have a plate ready. Carefully lift the salmon from the slow cooker by grasping the parchment on both sides, tilting the paper slightly as you lift to drain off the liquid. Serve immediately, or cool and refrigerate.

Mix the yoghurt, honey and spice paste then add enough cold water to form a pouring consistency and season to taste.

Serve the salmon with yoghurt sauce, green salad and brown rice sprinkled with spiced cashew and pumpkin seed trail mix (see p. 148).

INGREDIENTS

1 handful leftover raw vegetables (any end pieces of fennel, carrot, celery, onions or spring onion) or 1 organic carrot and 1 celery stick, rinsed and roughly chopped

1 star anise

1 tbsp coriander seeds

1 tbsp whole black peppercorns

1 (600g) piece skin-on salmon fillet

350 ml water

1 tbsp organic cider vinegar

1 tbsp sea salt

150ml probiotic yoghurt

1 tsp honey

2 tbsp yellow spice paste (see p. 107)

LENTIL AND PORK LASAGNE

INGREDIENTS

400g pork mince

extra virgin olive oil

800ml tomato sugo (see p. 102)

400g dried lentils, rinsed and
picked through

800ml water mixed with

2 chicken or veg stock pots

1 bay leaf

2 tbsp red spice paste (see p.
104)

4 tbsp almost no-cook sauce
(see p. 185)

1 tsp chilli flakes

2 tbsp fresh thyme leaves

1 bulb roasted garlic

1 tsp ground cumin

4 tbsp feta cheese, crumbled

1 (300g) tub ricotta

200g fresh spinach leaves,
roughly chopped

570ml milk

25g plain flour

50g butter

a small piece of Parmesan rind

30g grated Parmesan cheese

250g fresh lasagne sheets

Using pork and lentils instead of beef for the sauce makes this a healthier version of the more traditional lasagne.

Brown the pork mince with 1 tbsp oil in a frying pan over a medium heat for 5 minutes, then put in the slow cooker. Add the sugo, lentils, stock, bay leaf, spice paste, tomato and olive sauce and chilli flakes and stir to combine. Cook on low for 4–5 hours, or until lentils have softened and sauce is thick. Once cooked, remove the bay leaf, add the thyme leaves and season to taste.

Squeeze the roasted garlic into a bowl and mix with the cumin and feta, then add the drained ricotta and spinach. Mix well, then season.

Put the milk in a saucepan, add the flour, butter and Parmesan rind and bring everything gradually up to simmering point over a medium heat, whisking continuously with a balloon whisk, until the sauce has thickened and become smooth and glossy. Watch it carefully – you don't want it to burn. Turn the heat down to its lowest setting and let the sauce cook gently for 5 minutes. Remove the rind, add in the grated Parmesan and season to taste.

If you want to eat this now, preheat your oven to 200°C.

Spoon half the meat sauce into the base of a ceramic lasagne dish then top with a layer of lasagne. Spoon on the ricotta/spinach mix then add another layer of pasta, spoon on the rest of the sauce then top with a final layer of pasta. Pour the white sauce evenly over the top. Cook in your preheated oven and bake for 30 minutes until golden and bubbling. If you're making ahead you can wrap and freeze it at this stage once it's cooled a bit.

TURKEY
CHILLI TACOS

Turkey mince is low in fat and full of protein. This super-tasty sauce tastes great layered with the other ingredients to create Mexican-style tacos. If you prefer, just ladle the chilli over brown rice in a bowl.

Sauté the spring onions and onion with the bell pepper for 3 minutes. Then squeeze in the garlic and add the spice paste, along with the turkey mince. Cook for a minute then transfer the mixture to the slow cooker. Add the tinned tomatoes, sugo, ketchup, kidney beans and cumin seeds. Stir to combine.

Cover and cook for 6–8 hours on low, or until the chilli thickens. Add the frozen sweetcorn and cook for 10 more minutes. The chilli can be frozen at this stage and defrosted when you need it.

When ready to eat, season and add hot sauce to taste. Layer up on the flatbreads or tortillas with cooked brown rice, grated cheese, DG pickles (see p. 144), low-fat crème fraîche, crisp lettuce, and roasted shallot and butterbean dip (see p. 139).

INGREDIENTS

6 spring onions, sliced on the diagonal

1 large yellow onion, peeled and diced

1 red pepper, deseeded and diced

1 bulb of roasted garlic

4 tbsp red spice paste (see p. 104)

800g turkey mince

2 400g tins of good-quality cherry or chopped tomatoes

400g tomato sugo (see p. 102)

4 tbsp DG ketchup (see p. 142)

1 400g tin kidney beans, drained

2 tsp cumin seeds

200g frozen sweetcorn

hot sauce to taste

super seeded flatbreads or wholemeal tortillas

EMERGENCY 10 MEALS

These are advance prep meals that are stored in the freezer to be pulled out and stir fried from frozen in under 10 minutes while you prepare an accompaniment. Make up a few Emergency 10 bags on your prep/shopping day and they will be ready to cook over the next fortnight. Easy!

EACH BAG SERVES 1

HOW TO ASSEMBLE
AN EMERGENCY 10 MEAL

* Chopped herbs
* Dressing ingredients
* Finely sliced raw vegetables
* Frozen vegetables
* Par-cooked chopped vegetables
* Cooked legumes, noodles or frozen prawns

PRAWN AND SPRING VEG SAUTÉ

INGREDIENTS

200g frozen Dublin Bay prawns, shelled and deveined

80g frozen petit pois

60g tender stem broccoli

60g young asparagus

60g green beans

2 handfuls fresh spinach

2 tbsp extra virgin olive oil

1 tsp ground cumin

2 tbsp wholegrain mustard

½ tsp chilli flakes

1 tsp manuka honey

4 tbsp fresh dill and flat-leaf parsley, chopped

100g quick-cook polenta

50g crumbled feta or blue cheese

1 tbsp extra virgin olive oil

This fresh-tasting sauté is great piled over cheesy polenta.

Divide the prawns and peas between two 1 litre reusable freezer bags. Cut the broccoli into quarters lengthwise through the stem, cut the asparagus on the diagonal, top and tail the green beans. Divide the broccoli, asparagus and green beans between the 2 bags with a handful of spinach in each bag. Mix the oil, cumin, mustard, chilli flakes, honey and herbs in a teacup then divide this between the 2 bags. Give the closed bag a quick shake to mix together.

Freeze immediately (for best results lay the bags flat in the freezer).

When you're ready to eat, heat a frying pan over medium heat, put in the frozen stir fry to and cook 6–8 minutes until the prawns are fully cooked (pink) and the vegetables are tender.

Serve with quick-cook polenta, laced with the cheese, olive oil and seasoning .

STEAK AND SOBA STIR FRY

INGREDIENTS

150g soba noodles

2 tbsp sesame oil

80g frozen soya beans

1 yellow pepper

60g baby corn

60g mangetout

1 courgette

1 head pak choi, sliced

3 tbsp soy sauce

juice of ½ a lime

3 cloves of roasted garlic

2cm ginger, peeled and grated

1 tsp tahini

a small handful of fresh
coriander leaves

1 300g sirloin or striploin steak
(for when you're ready to cook)

This fragrant noodle dish packed with vegetables is topped with tender, griddled steak slices.

Bring a pot of unsalted water to the boil, add the noodles then reduce to simmer and cook for 6–7 minutes. Blanch in cold water, drain and dress with 1 tsp of the sesame oil.

Divide the noodles and beans between two 1 litre reusable freezer bags. Cut the yellow pepper into 1cm slices, cut the corn and mangetout on the diagonal and spiralise the courgette or slice it very thinly. Divide the yellow pepper, corn, mangetout and courgette between the 2 bags with a handful of sliced pak choi in each bag.

Mix the remaining sesame oil with 2 tablespoons of the soy sauce, lime juice, roasted garlic, ginger, tahini and coriander in a teacup then divide this between the 2 bags. Give the closed bag a quick shake to mix together.

Freeze immediately (for best results lay the bags flat in the freezer).

To make the meal, rub the steak with the olive oil and 1 tbsp soy sauce. Heat a heavy frying pan over medium heat, put in the steak and cook for 5 minutes for medium-rare, or to your liking, turning every minute. Remove the steak to a warm plate to rest. Turn up the pan to hot, add the frozen stir fry to the pan and cook for 5 minutes or until the vegetables are tender and the noodles warmed.

Slice the steak and serve on top of the stir fry and noodles.

PAN-FRIED COCONUT SQUASH AND SEABASS

Freshly sautéed seabass tastes great piled over the spicy veg and beans.

Preheat oven to 200°C.

Put the butternut squash on a baking tray and bake for 35 minutes. Remove from the oven and allow to cool. Using a dessert spoon, scoop out mounds of squash.

Divide the squash scoops and beans between two 1 litre freezer bags and add a handful of kale to each bag. Mix 1 tbsp olive oil with the coconut milk, tomato sugo, spice paste and mint in a teacup, then divide this between the 2 bags. Give the closed bags a quick shake to mix together.

Freeze immediately (for best results lay the bags flat in the freezer).

When you're ready to eat, put a heavy frying pan over a medium heat, tip in the frozen stir fry and cook for 6–8 minutes, stirring frequently, or until the vegetables are tender and the beans warmed. In a separate pan heat 1 tbsp oil on a medium heat and cook the fish for 2 minutes on each side.

Serve the fish on the squash and beans with a squeeze of lime.

INGREDIENTS

½ a butternut squash

1 400g tin cannellini beans, drained

2 handfuls of baby kale, rinsed and chopped

light olive oil

4 tbsp coconut milk

4 tbsp tomato sugo (see p. 102)

2 tbsp yellow spice paste (see p. 107)

2 tbsp fresh mint, chopped

2 fillets seabass (for when you're ready to cook)

juice of ½ a lime

BALSAMIC, PARMESAN AND CAULIFLOWER GRIDDLED PORK

This dinner is packed with punchy flavours of mustard, garlic, Parmesan and herbs.

Bring a pot of salted water to boil, add the cauliflower, then reduce to a simmer and cook for 6–7 minutes. Blanch in cold water and drain.

Divide the florets and peas between two 1 litre freezer bags. Then divide the spring onion between the bags, along with the spinach, rocket and rosemary. In a teacup, mix 3 tbsp of olive oil with the vinegar, squeezed-out roasted garlic, mustard, Parmesan and thyme, then divide this between the 2 bags. Give the closed bag a quick shake to mix together.

Freeze immediately (for best results lay the bags flat in the freezer).

When you're ready to cook, add the frozen stir fry to a pan over a medium heat and cook for 8 minutes, stirring frequently, or until the vegetables are tender and warmed. In a separate pan over a medium heat cook the pork steaks for 3 minutes each side in 1 tbsp olive oil.

Serve the pork sliced over the stir fry. Dollop some almost no-cook sauce over each serving.

INGREDIENTS

1 cauliflower, broken into florets

100g frozen petit pois

3 spring onions, sliced on the diagonal

2 handfuls baby spinach

1 handful rocket

2 sprigs rosemary

extra virgin olive oil

1 tbsp balsamic vinegar

½ bulb roasted garlic

1 tsp wholegrain mustard

120g Parmesan cheese, grated

1 tbsp fresh thyme leaves

2 thin pork steaks (for when you're ready to cook)

almost no-cook sauce (see pp. 185–189), to serve

These nutritionally dense but light supper meals make great use of the basic broth (see p. 108).

EACH MEAL SERVES 2

MINESTRONE BEAN BROTH

INGREDIENTS

½ a small leek, washed and sliced

1 small carrot, peeled and diced

1 stalk celery, diced

½ courgette, diced

1 tbsp extra virgin olive oil

1 garlic clove, peeled

500ml basic broth (see p. 108)

100ml tomato sugo (see p. 102)

2 sprigs rosemary

1 400g tin cannellini beans

3 tbsp fresh flat-leaf parsley

2 tbsp Parmesan, grated

Delicious with a swirl of seasonal almost no-cook sauce (see p. 185–189) and a sprinkling of crispy bacon.

Put the leek, carrot, celery and courgette in a saucepan with the olive oil and sauté gently over a medium heat for 4 minutes. Grate in the garlic clove, cook for a further 2 minutes then pour in the broth and simmer for 10 minutes. Add the sugo, rosemary and drained beans and cook for a further 5 minutes. Remove the rosemary, ladle into deep bowls and serve with sprinkled with parsley and Parmesan.

LEMONY RICE BROTH

This dish is adapted from an old Italian recipe. It is delicious as is or as a great base for carrying leftovers like shredded chicken, cooked prawns or chopped veg.

Put the basic broth, lemon juice and zest in a small saucepan over a medium heat.

Whisk eggs, crushed garlic and Parmesan cheese together in a glass jug.

When the broth is bubbling, add the egg mixture in a slow stream, whisking the broth rapidly to incorporate. Reduce the heat to a simmer, add the greens (with any leftovers) to the broth and cook for another 2 to 3 minutes.

Pour the broth over bowls of brown rice.

INGREDIENTS

500ml basic broth
(see p. 108)
zest and juice of ½ a lemon
2 small free-range eggs
1 clove of garlic, peeled and
crushed
2 tbsp grated Parmesan
2 handfuls of fresh seasonal
greens (watercress, spinach,
baby kale)
150g cooked brown rice
(defrosted or cooked fresh)

RAMEN SOBA NOODLE BROTH

INGREDIENTS

2 free-range eggs

2 tbsp low sodium soy sauce

150g soba noodles

1 tbsp light olive oil

100g large flat (Portobello) mushrooms, thinly sliced

3 spring onions, sliced on the diagonal

2 tbsp yellow spice paste (see p. 107)

500ml basic broth (see p. 108)

1 tbsp miso paste

160g free-range chicken breast

a handful baby pak choi, sliced into quarters lengthwise

Add hot sauce or sriracha to spice up this filling dish.

Place the eggs in a small pan and add enough cold water to cover them by about 1cm. Bring the water up to boiling point then turn down to a simmer for 7 minutes. Remove from the pan with a slotted spoon then let the cold tap run over them for about 1 minute. Allow to cool and then peel and dress with soy sauce.

Cook the noodles in a pot of unsalted water for 6–7 minutes, then blanch in cold water and drain. Set aside.

Heat the oil in a large pan over a medium heat and sauté the mushrooms and spring onions for about 5 minutes until softened. Add the spice paste and basic broth and bring to a simmer. Stir in the miso, then add the chicken breast and cook for 15 minutes. Remove the chicken and shred it with two forks. Add it back to the broth along with the pak choi and noodles. Remove from the heat and serve each portion with a halved soy sauce egg.

GREEN LENTIL, KALE AND CHORIZO BROTH

Add a poached or fried egg on top of this hearty broth as an extra treat and protein fix.

Heat the oil in a saucepan, add the leek and sauté gently for 5 minutes over a medium heat. Add the chorizo to the pan along with the roasted garlic and spice paste and cook for a further 5 minutes. Add the lentils and broth and cook for another 5 minutes. Add the kale, allow to wilt then serve the broth in deep bowls. Finish with a sprinkle of crumbled feta.

INGREDIENTS

2 tablespoons olive oil

1 small leek, washed and sliced

150g chorizo, sliced

2 cloves roasted garlic

1 tbsp red spice paste
(see p. 104)

200g cooked green
speckled lentils

500ml basic broth (see p. 108)

2 handfuls baby kale, rinsed
and chopped

2 tbsp crumbled feta cheese

DESSERT

Eating well doesn't have to mean skipping dessert at every meal. Its all about balance and moderation, so if you fancy a small dessert, have it, but maybe look at enjoying it on days you have trained and aim to keep it to every other day.

WHIPPED COCONUT CREAM

Thoroughly shake the tin of coconut milk and chill it in the fridge overnight (if you're short on time pop in the freezer for 1–2 hours). Carefully spoon out the thicker coconut cream, reserving the thinner liquid in the tin.

Whisk the coconut cream until soft peaks form. The cream may get thicker once whipped and kept in the fridge, but stirring in a tbsp of the reserved thinner liquid will bring it back to soft peaks.

INGREDIENTS
1 400ml tin of full-fat coconut milk

MAKES 400ML CREAM

COCO-CHOC BARS

INGREDIENTS

50g coconut flour

150g desiccated coconut

300ml full-fat coconut milk

2 tbsp maple syrup

200g 70% dark chocolate,
broken into pieces

MAKES 18 BARS

My healthy take on the Bounty Bar is a great pick-me-up or post-workout treat.

In a large bowl mix the flour, desiccated coconut, coconut milk and maple syrup.

With wet hands shape the mixture into 18 bars and arrange them on a wire rack on a baking tray. Refrigerate for 1 hour or pop in the freezer for 10–15 minutes.

Put 150g of the chocolate pieces in a microwaveable bowl. Set the microwave at half power then melt the chocolate in 30-second bursts to start with, reducing to 10-second bursts, stirring between each burst until the chocolate is almost melted with a few small chunks remaining. Remove the bowl from the microwave then stir in the remaining chocolate piece by piece until the chocolate cools and thickens slightly.

Pour the chocolate over the bars and leave to cool uncovered. These bars will keep for a week in the fridge (if you can keep your hands off them for that long!).

DAIRY-FREE CHOCOLATE MOUSSE

INGREDIENTS

150g 70% dark chocolate

6 free-range egg whites (use pasteurised egg white in a carton for ease)

½ tsp organic cider vinegar or lemon juice

3 rounded tbsp unrefined golden caster sugar

coconut cream, to serve

SERVES 6

This rich dinner party-style dessert is packed with antioxidants. Serve with fresh blueberries or raspberries.

Break the chocolate into pieces and place into a large microwaveable bowl. Set the microwave at half power then melt the chocolate in 30-second bursts to start with, then reducing to 10-second bursts, stirring between each burst until the chocolate is melted. Leave to cool at room temperature for 10 minutes.

Whisk the egg whites and vinegar/lemon juice in a large, clean bowl until they form soft peaks. Add the sugar and continue to whisk until firm peaks form.

Vigorously whisk one-third of this mixture into the liquid chocolate until thick and well combined. Then gently fold the remaining egg whites into the chocolate mixture, using a spatula, until all of the egg white has been incorporated into the chocolate. Chill in individual glasses for 2–3 hours in the fridge then top with whipped coconut cream (see p. 230).

This mousse also makes a delicious ganache-style icing for cakes and cupcakes.

DAIRY-FREE ICE-CREAM SUNDAES

An adaptable sweet treat enjoyed by adults as much as kids. You can play around with the toppings – I've added some suggestions.

INGREDIENTS

6 very ripe bananas, peeled and cut into bite-sized pieces

MAKES 6 SUNDAES

Put the banana pieces in an airtight container and freeze for at least 2 hours but ideally overnight.

In a food processor blitz the frozen banana pieces. Don't worry if it looks crumbly at first, keep blending! Scrape down the food processor, and blend again until completely smooth.

Transfer to an airtight container and freeze for 2 hours.

Pop the ice-cream into glass tumblers and drizzle over three-step compote (see p. 110) slightly warmed choc-hazelnut butter (see p. 153) or maple caramel (see p. 238) Then add your fresh fruit of choice, sweet trail mix (see p. 150) and a dollop of whipped coconut cream (see p. 230)

HAZELNUT COCOA SQUARES

These delicious squares are an indulgent way to use the choc-hazelnut butter (see p. 153). They are packed with energy so are great as a post-workout snack.

Line a 20cm square baking tin with baking parchment.

Gently crush the roasted hazelnuts with the back of a wooden spoon then sprinkle into the bottom of the tin.

Put the honey, chia seeds, coconut oil, tahini, vanilla extract and salt in a small pot on a medium-low heat. Stir until everything is melted. Let cool for a couple of minutes then pour the mixture over the hazelnuts in the tin. Place in the fridge for about 30 minutes to set.

Remove the baking tray from the fridge, spread over the choc-hazelnut butter and return to chill in the fridge for 15 minutes.

Break up 150g of the chocolate and place in a micro-waveable bowl. Set the microwave at half power then melt the chocolate in 30-second bursts to start with, reducing to 10-second bursts and stirring between each burst until the chocolate is almost melted with a few small chunks remaining. Remove the bowl from the microwave then stir in the remaining chocolate piece by piece, stirring until the chocolate cools and thickens slightly. Pour the chocolate over the mixture in the tin and leave to set in a cool place.

Cut into 20 4cm by 5cm bars and store in the fridge for up to a week.

INGREDIENTS

100g roasted hazelnuts

120ml honey

60g milled chia seeds

100g coconut oil

120g tahini

1 tsp vanilla extract

a pinch of sea salt

150g choc-hazelnut butter (see p. 153)

200g 70% dark cooking chocolate, broken into pieces

MAKES 20 SQUARES

NO-BAKE CARAMEL CHOCOLATE BARS

Make triple the amount of maple caramel and store in a glass jar in the fridge for up to 2 weeks.

Line a 20cm square baking tin with baking parchment.

In a small bowl mix together the base layer ingredients with a wooden spoon to a soft dough. With the back of a spoon, press the dough into the tin in an even layer. Pop in the fridge while you make the caramel.

In a small pot melt the caramel ingredients on a medium heat for about 3 minutes while gently stirring. Allow to cool a little, then pour over the base layer. Place in the fridge for about 30 minutes to set.

Remove from the tin, cut into 2.5cm x 5cm bars and pop them on a wire cooling rack over a shallow baking tray.

Break up 150g of chocolate and place into a micro-waveable bowl. Set the microwave at half power then melt the chocolate in 30-second bursts to start with, reducing to 10-second bursts and stirring between each burst until the chocolate is almost melted with a few small chunks remaining. Remove the bowl from the microwave, then stir in the remaining chocolate piece by piece, stirring until the chocolate cools and thickens slightly. Pour the chocolate over the bars and leave to cool uncovered in a cool place.

Store in the fridge for up to a week. You can also make this in a 23cm round tin, sprinkle with some extra sea salt and serve as a dessert tart.

INGREDIENTS

FOR THE BASE LAYER:

120g coconut flour

60ml maple syrup

60ml treacle or molasses

75g melted coconut oil

2 tbsp chia seeds

1 tsp vanilla extract

FOR THE MAPLE CARAMEL LAYER:

60ml maple syrup

50g coconut oil

60g almond butter

1 tsp caramel extract

a pinch of sea salt

200g 70% dark chocolate

MAKES 40 BARS

'ALL ROUNDER' CAKE MIX

INGREDIENTS

100g stoneground unbleached
plain flour

100g coconut flour or
buckwheat flour

60g ground chia seeds

120g ground almonds

2½ tsp baking powder

4 large free-range eggs

200g caster sugar

200ml light olive oil

1 tsp vanilla extract

260ml buttermilk

MAKES 1 CAKE

This is a great recipe that can be used to make sponges, cupcakes and blondie bars. You could also use it to make a fruit and nut loaf cake by mixing in 2 tablespoons of sweet trail mix (see p. 150) and baking in a loaf tin.

Preheat the oven to 180°C. Grease and line a 23cm springform pan, 20cm square pan or cupcake tin.

Mix the dry ingredients, apart from the sugar, together in a bowl.

In another bowl, whisk the eggs, add the sugar and mix until well combined. Add the olive oil and whisk until the mix has thickened slightly. Finally stir in the vanilla and buttermilk.

Add the dry ingredients to the bowl and mix until a smooth batter is formed. Pour the batter into the prepared tin/cupcake tray, and bake for 30–45 minutes, or 15 minutes for the cupcakes.

You will know the cake is done when it has begun to pull away from the sides of the pan and springs back lightly when touched. Allow the cake to cool for 10 minutes in the pan, then gently remove it and allow it to cool completely on a rack.

Serve with three-step compote (see p. 110) and whipped coconut cream (see p. 230) for an afternoon treat.

ST CLEMENTS DRIZZLE CAKE

Substitute the juice of ½ a lemon and 1 orange for the buttermilk, add the zest of each and substitute peppery extra virgin olive oil for the light olive oil.

Make an easy icing with the rest of the lemon juice and a couple of spoons of icing sugar.

RICH CHOCOLATE CAKE

Instead of 200ml olive oil, use 100ml melted coconut oil and 100ml olive oil, substitute light brown sugar for the caster sugar and use 50g cocoa powder and only 50g coconut flour.

Top with the dairy-free chocolate mousse (see p. 233).

DOUBLE CHOC SPELT BLONDIES

Line a 28cm x 18cm brownie tin, substitute spelt flour for the plain flour, muscovado sugar for the caster sugar and use almond rather than buttermilk.

Swirl in 2 tbsp choc-hazelnut butter (see p. 153) and 1 tbsp chocolate chunks before baking for 25 minutes. Remove and leave to cool in the tin for 10 minutes. Delicious served warm with banana ice-cream (see p. 234). Below are some variations for other delicious blondie combos. In each case, add instead of the choc-hazelnut butter and chocolate chunks.

* Add 1 tbsp maple caramel (see p. 238) and 1 tbsp ricotta for Caramel Cheesecake Blondies.
* Add 2 tbsp no-cook compote (see p. 110) for Very Berry Blondies.
* Add 1 tbsp maple caramel (see p. 238), 1 tbsp chopped white chocolate and 1 tbsp chopped banana for Banoffee Blondies.
* Add 2 tbsp sweet trail mix (see p. 150) for Fruit & Nut Blondies.

INDEX